# Folens

# MATHS

## Programme

GW00599144

Folens Publishers

## ACKNOWLEDGEMENTS

**Author Team:**

Sue Briggs

Rosemary Flower

Don Gee

Dr Bob Hartman

Carole Martin

Lorna Mulhern

Peter Ransom

Caroline Starkey

Biff Vernon

Susan Ball

Russell Robshaw

**Series Consultant:**

Margaret Mackenzie

**Project Director:**

Mary Pardoe

United Kingdom: Folens Publishers, Apex Business Centre, Boscombe Road, Dunstable, LU5 4RL.
Email: folens@folens.com

Ireland: Folens Publishers, Greenhills Road, Tallaght, Dublin 24.
Email: info@folens.ie

Poland: JUKA, ul. Renesansowa 38, Warsaw 01-905.

Editors: Maggie Cameron and Mairi Sutherland
Design and layout: FMS Design for Education
Cover design: Duncan McTeer
Illustrations:
Debbie Clark, cartoon on page 85: Duncan McTeer
Photographs:
cover: Benedict Luxmoore/www.arcaid.co.uk and Grant Smith/Corbis
page 55: *Equivalent VIII*, Carl Andre, 1966 © Tate, London, 2002.
© Carl Andre/VAGA, New York/DACS, London 2002.

First published 2002 by Folens Limited. Based on the Folens Maths Programme (Teacher Files) published 2001–2002.

ISBN 1 84303 349-6

# Contents

# Contents

# Contents

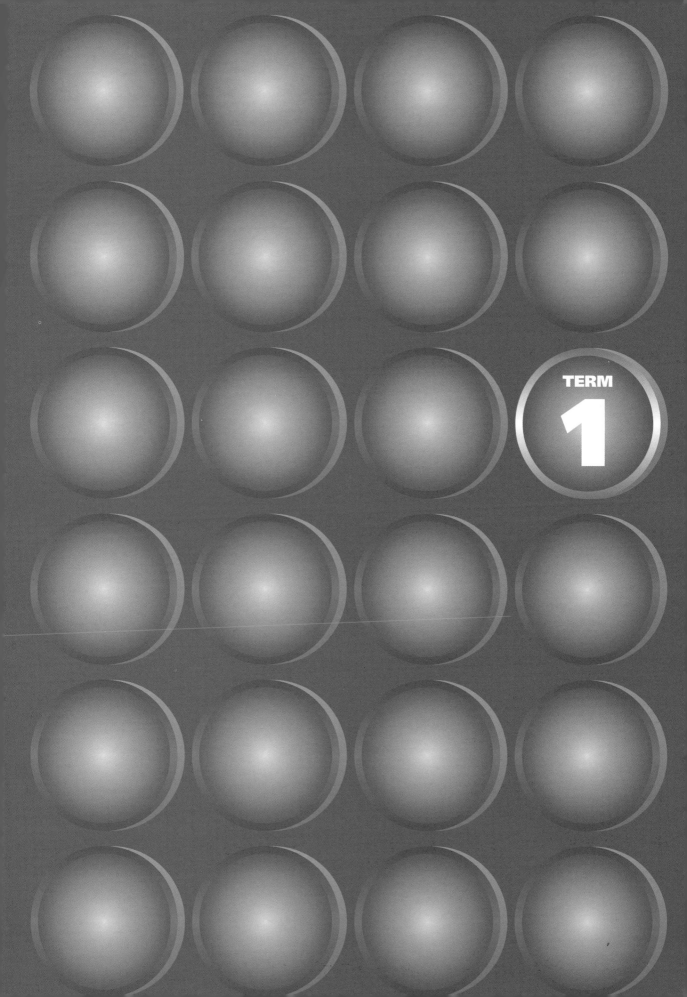

**TERM 1**

# Unit 1
# Magic squares

## Lesson 1  It's magic

In a magic square the numbers are arranged so that each horizontal row, vertical column and diagonal have the same total. This is called the 'magic total'.

In a 3 by 3 magic square this magic total is always equal to 3 times the number at the centre.

A magic square

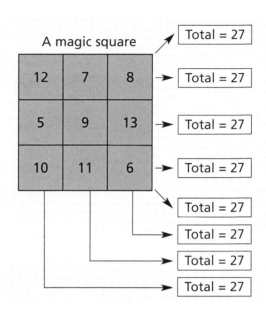

| 12 | 7 | 8 |
|----|---|---|
| 5 | 9 | 13 |
| 10 | 11 | 6 |

Total = 27
Total = 27
Total = 27
Total = 27
Total = 27
Total = 27
Total = 27
Total = 27

## Activity

**1.** Which of these are magic squares?

Square A

| 12 | 8 | 7 |
|----|---|---|
| 4 | 9 | 14 |
| 11 | 10 | 6 |

Square B

| 22 | 6 | 20 |
|----|---|----|
| 13 | 16 | 18 |
| 12 | 26 | 10 |

Square C

| 16 | 2 | 12 |
|----|---|----|
| 6 | 10 | 14 |
| 8 | 17 | 4 |

Square D

| 17 | 18 | 13 |
|----|----|----|
| 12 | 16 | 20 |
| 19 | 14 | 15 |

**2.** Copy and complete these magic squares. It will help to find the magic total for each one first.

Square E

| 20 | 6 | |
|----|---|---|
| | 14 | |
| | 22 | |

Square F

| | | 24 |
|---|---|----|
| | 15 | |
| 6 | | 18 |

Square G

| 22 | | |
|----|---|---|
| 7 | 13 | 19 |
| | | |

Square H

| 16 | | 36 |
|----|---|----|
| | | |
| 6 | 31 | 26 |

magic total = ?    magic total = ?    magic total = ?    magic total = ?

| | | |
|---|---|---|
| 8 | 1 | 6 |
| 3 | 5 | 7 |
| 4 | 9 | 2 |

This magic square uses each of the numbers 1–9.

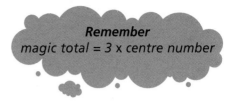

*Remember*
*magic total = 3 x centre number*

**3.**  a. Copy and complete this list of the first nine odd numbers:

1, 3, 5, ____, ____, ____, ____, ____, ____.

b. Copy and complete this magic square using these odd numbers.

| | | |
|---|---|---|
| | | |
| | 9 | |
| | | 3 |

**4.**  Finish each list of the first nine terms.
Then make a magic square from each list.

a. 10, 12, 14, 16, ____, ____, ____, ____, ____.

b. 12, 15, 18, 21, ____, ____, ____, ____, ____.

**Challenge**

**5.**  a. Copy and complete this number sequence:

3, 7, 11, 15, ____, ____, ____, ____, ____.

b. Make a magic square using these nine numbers.

**6.**  For each of these sequences make a magic square using the first nine terms.

a. 56, 60, 64, 68, ____, ____, ____, ____, ____.

b. 48, 43, 38, 33, ____, ____, ____, ____, ____.

## Lesson 2  Make magic

This magic square represents an infinite number of different magic squares. Each different value of $n$ will give a different square. The magic total for this 3 x 3 magic square is $3n + 3 = 3 (n + 1)$.

A magic square

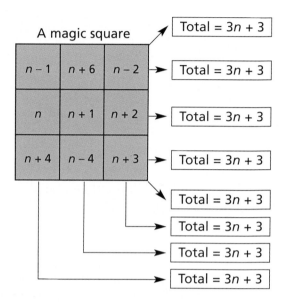

| $n - 1$ | $n + 6$ | $n - 2$ |
| $n$ | $n + 1$ | $n + 2$ |
| $n + 4$ | $n - 4$ | $n + 3$ |

Total = $3n + 3$
Total = $3n + 3$
Total = $3n + 3$
Total = $3n + 3$
Total = $3n + 3$
Total = $3n + 3$
Total = $3n + 3$
Total = $3n + 3$

### Activity

Square A

| $n + 3$ | $n + 14$ | $n + 4$ |
| $n + 8$ | $n + 7$ | $n + 6$ |
| $n + 10$ | $n$ | $n + 11$ |

1. Using square A, make magic squares with the following values:

   a. $n = 3$

   b. $n = 5$

   c. $n = 8$

2. Which of these are magic squares?

Square B

| $n + 5$ | $n + 6$ | $n + 1$ |
| $n$ | $n + 4$ | $n + 8$ |
| $n + 7$ | $n + 2$ | $n + 3$ |

Square C

| $n + 4$ | $n + 18$ | $n + 8$ |
| $n + 14$ | $n + 10$ | $n + 6$ |
| $n + 12$ | $n + 2$ | $n + 16$ |

Square D

| $n + 3$ | $n + 14$ | $n + 4$ |
| $n + 8$ | $n + 7$ | $n + 6$ |
| $n + 13$ | $n$ | $n + 11$ |

**3.** Copy and complete these magic squares.

Square E

| $n + 11$ | | $n + 3$ |
|---|---|---|
| | $n + 9$ | |
| | | $n + 7$ |

magic total =    ?

Square F

| $n + 8$ | $n + 15$ | $n + 7$ |
|---|---|---|
| | $n + 10$ | |
| | | |

magic total =    ?

Square G

| $n + 8$ | | $n + 6$ |
|---|---|---|
| $n + 3$ | | |
| $n + 4$ | | |

magic total =    ?

## Challenge

**4.** Is this a magic square?

Square H

| $n - 2$ | $n + 9$ | $n - 1$ |
|---|---|---|
| $n + 3$ | $n + 2$ | $n + 1$ |
| $n + 5$ | $n - 5$ | $n + 6$ |

**5.** Copy and complete these magic squares.

Square I

| | | $n - 4$ |
|---|---|---|
| | | |
| $n + 2$ | $n - 3$ | $n - 2$ |

Square J

| $2n + 20$ | | |
|---|---|---|
| $2n$ | | |
| $5n + 4$ | 24 | |

**6.** a. Show that K and L are both magic squares.

b. What value of $n$ gives these squares the same magic total?

Square K

| $2n + 3$ | $2n + 5$ | $2n - 5$ |
|---|---|---|
| $2n - 7$ | $2n + 1$ | $2n + 9$ |
| $2n + 7$ | $2n - 3$ | $2n - 1$ |

Square L

| $n + 6$ | $n + 4$ | $n - 1$ |
|---|---|---|
| $n - 4$ | $n + 3$ | $n + 10$ |
| $n + 7$ | $n + 2$ | $n$ |

# Unit 1
# Magic squares

## Lesson 3  Magic solutions

Square A

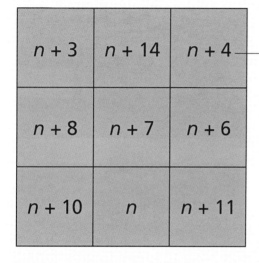

| $n + 3$ | $n + 14$ | $n + 4$ |
| --- | --- | --- |
| $n + 8$ | $n + 7$ | $n + 6$ |
| $n + 10$ | $n$ | $n + 11$ |

It is important to match the given value to the correct expression.

When the value of $n$ has been found the magic square can be completed by substitution.

Use square A to make a magic square with the top right-hand number equal to 10.

$n + 4 = 10$

$n \xrightarrow{\boxed{+ 4}} 10$

$6 \xleftarrow{\boxed{- 4}} 10$

So $n = 6$

This gives the magic square:

| 9 | 20 | 10 |
| --- | --- | --- |
| 14 | 13 | 12 |
| 16 | 6 | 17 |

---

## Activity

Square B

| $n + 5$ | $n + 6$ | $n + 1$ |
| --- | --- | --- |
| $n$ | $n + 4$ | $n + 8$ |
| $n + 7$ | $n + 2$ | $n + 3$ |

1. Square B is a magic square.

   a. Add the expressions in each line to find the magic total for this square.

   b. Complete this magic square using $n = 6$.

   $n + 1 = 6 + 1$
   $= 7$ → 7

   | | | 7 |
   | --- | --- | --- |
   | | | |
   | 13 | | |

   $n + 7 = 6 + 7$
   $= 13$ → 13

c. These magic squares were made using square B. For each square, find the value of *n* and use your value of *n* to complete the magic square. Show your working in your exercise book.

Square 1

| 8 | | |
|---|---|---|
| | | |
| | | |

Square 2

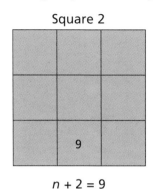

Square 3

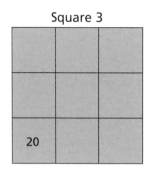

*n* + 5 = 8

*n* ⟶ 8

⟵ 8

So *n* =

*n* + 2 = 9

*n* ⟶

⟵

So *n* =

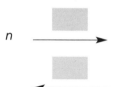

*n* ⟶

⟵

So *n* =

2. Use number machines to solve each equation.

a.
| 5*x* + 4 = 39 |
|---|

Input        Output

*x* ⟶<sup>× 5</sup> ⟶<sup>+ 4</sup> 39

⟵<sup>÷ 5</sup> ⟵<sup>− 4</sup> 39

b.
| 7*x* + 2 = 23 |
|---|

Input        Output

*x* ⟶<sup>× 7</sup> ⟶<sup>+ 2</sup> 23

⟵<sup>÷ 7</sup> ⟵<sup>− 2</sup> 23

c.
| 4*x* − 2 = 34 |
|---|

Input        Output

*x* ⟶<sup>× 4</sup> ⟶<sup>− 2</sup> 34

⟵<sup>÷ 4</sup> ⟵<sup>+ 2</sup> 34

### Challenge

3. Use the expressions in square C to complete each of these magic squares.
You will need to work out the value of *n* and substitute your value of *n* in each expression.

Square C

| 3*n* + 1 | 7*n* + 4 | 2*n* + 4 |
|---|---|---|
| 6 + 3*n* | 4*n* + 3 | 5*n* |
| 6*n* + 2 | *n* + 2 | 5*n* + 5 |

Square 4

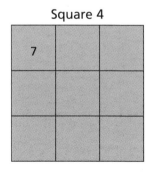

| 7 | | |
|---|---|---|
| | | |
| | | |

Square 5

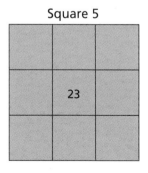

| | | |
|---|---|---|
| | 23 | |
| | | |

4. Use number machines to solve these equations.

a. 3*x* − 7 = 23

b. 7*x* − 6 = 36

c. 6 + 6*x* = 42

c. These magic squares were made using square B. For each square, find the value of *n* and use your value of *n* to complete the magic square. Show your working in your exercise book.

Square 1

| 8 | | |
|---|---|---|
| | | |
| | | |

Square 2

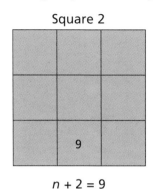

Square 3

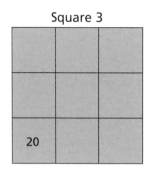

$n + 5 = 8$

$n \xrightarrow{+5} 8$

$\xleftarrow{\phantom{xxx}} 8$

So $n =$

$n + 2 = 9$

$n \xrightarrow{\phantom{xxx}}$

$\xleftarrow{\phantom{xxx}}$

So $n =$

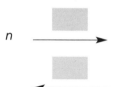

$n \xrightarrow{\phantom{xxx}}$

$\xleftarrow{\phantom{xxx}}$

So $n =$

2. Use number machines to solve each equation.

a.
| $5x + 4 = 39$ |
|---|

Input        Output

$x \xrightarrow{\times 5} \xrightarrow{+4} 39$

$\xleftarrow{\div 5} \xleftarrow{-4} 39$

b.
| $7x + 2 = 23$ |
|---|

Input        Output

$x \xrightarrow{\times 7} \xrightarrow{+2} 23$

$\xleftarrow{\div 7} \xleftarrow{-2} 23$

c.
| $4x - 2 = 34$ |
|---|

Input        Output

$x \xrightarrow{\times 4} \xrightarrow{-2} 34$

$\xleftarrow{\div 4} \xleftarrow{+2} 34$

### Challenge

3. Use the expressions in square C to complete each of these magic squares.
You will need to work out the value of *n* and substitute your value of *n* in each expression.

Square C

| $3n + 1$ | $7n + 4$ | $2n + 4$ |
|---|---|---|
| $6 + 3n$ | $4n + 3$ | $5n$ |
| $6n + 2$ | $n + 2$ | $5n + 5$ |

Square 4

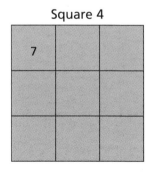

| 7 | | |
|---|---|---|
| | | |
| | | |

Square 5

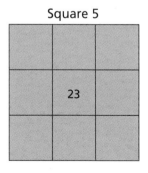

| | | |
|---|---|---|
| | 23 | |
| | | |

4. Use number machines to solve these equations.

a. $3x - 7 = 23$

b. $7x - 6 = 36$

c. $6 + 6x = 42$

# Unit 1
# Magic squares

## Lesson 4  More magic

**Evaluating expressions**

When putting values into an expression remember to multiply or divide before adding or subtracting.

---

**Activity**

1. Use the expressions in square A to complete these magic squares.
   One value is filled in for you on each square.

Square A

| | | |
|---|---|---|
| $x + y$ | $x + 2z$ | $x + 2y + z$ |
| $x + 2y + 2z$ | $x + y + z$ | $x$ |
| $x + z$ | $x + 2y$ | $x + y + 2z$ |

Square 1
$x = 2,\ y = 5,\ z = 1$

| 7 | | |
|---|---|---|
| | | |
| | | |

Square 2
$x = 4,\ y = 1,\ z = 3$

| | | |
|---|---|---|
| | | |
| 7 | | |

Square 3
$x = 8,\ y = 3,\ z = 4$

| | | 18 |
|---|---|---|
| | | |
| | | |

**Birthday magic**

2. You can use a date of birth to make a magic square.

   For example:

   16 April 1988 (16/4/88)

   $d = 16$, $m = 4$, $y = 88$.

   a. Complete the magic square for the date: 16 April 1988.

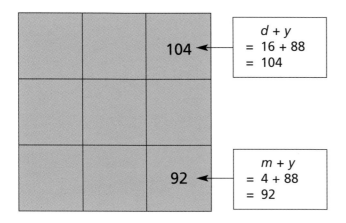

| | | 104 |
|---|---|---|
| | | |
| | | 92 |

$d + y$
$= 16 + 88$
$= 104$

$m + y$
$= 4 + 88$
$= 92$

| $2d + y + m$ | $y + 2m$ | $d + y$ |
|---|---|---|
| $y$ | $d + y + m$ | $y + 2d + 2m$ |
| $y + d + 2m$ | $2d + y$ | $m + y$ |

   b. Make a magic square for your own date of birth.

# Unit 2
# Rockets

## Lesson 1  Collecting data

In a practical class activity you will have made a rocket like the one shown here and used it to investigate whether the diameter of a rocket has an effect on how far it travels.

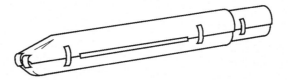

The table below shows the results collected by one group of pupils. They made four rockets, each with a different diameter, and fired each rocket five times. They measured the distance from launch to touchdown each time.

| Rocket | Diameter | Distance Travelled | | | | |
|--------|----------|-------|-------|-------|-------|-------|
| A | 2cm | 1.18m | 2.71m | 1.64m | 2.71m | 3.80m |
| B | 2.5cm | 2.30m | 1.50m | 2.91m | 2.02m | 2.30m |
| C | 3cm | 3.20m | 2.95m | 3.71m | 3.02m | 3.71m |
| D | 4cm | 1.94m | 2.70m | 1.40m | 1.94m | 1.42m |

**Activity**

1.  Compare these results with your own.

2.  Discuss anything that could have been done to improve the quality of the data.

# Lesson 2  Representing data

We often need to find the mode, median, mean and range of data.

*Remember:*
*The **mode** is the value that occurs most often.*
*The **median** is the number that appears in the middle if the numbers are arranged in order.*
*The **mean** can be found by adding the numbers and dividing the total by the number of the data.*
*The **range** is the difference between the largest and smallest values.*

We can draw graphs to represent the data. This helps us to compare and interpret the data.

## Activity

1.  Using your own results or the results in the table in Lesson 1,

    a.  find the mode, median and range of the data for each rocket

    b.  calculate the mean for each rocket.

2.  Work with others in your group to produce a poster describing the results. The poster should include a graph showing the results.

# Lesson 3  Using ICT

Graphical calculators can be used to analyse data. Computer spreadsheets are also useful. You can use them to perform calculations and to draw graphs.

## Activity

1.  Use a graphical calculator or computer spreadsheet to check your calculations in Lesson 2.

2.  Explore the facilities on your calculator or spreadsheet to draw bar graphs, pie charts, pictograms and scatter diagrams.

# Unit 3
# Zero to one

## Lesson 1  Zero to one

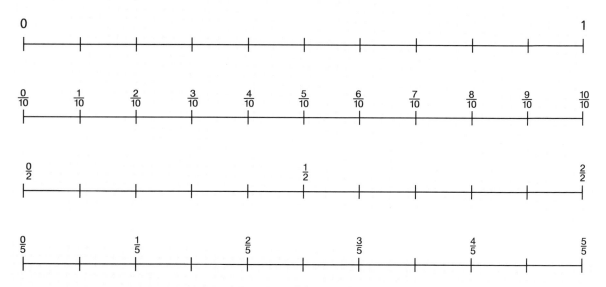

The diagram shows a 'zero to one' number line divided into 10 parts.

On one line 0 is recorded as $\frac{0}{10}$ (this means zero tenths) and 1 is recorded as $\frac{10}{10}$ (this means ten tenths).

This number line shows three different 'families' of fractions: 'tenths', 'halves' and 'fifths'.

### Activity

Your teacher will give you worksheets containing 'zero to one' number lines, each divided into a different number of parts.

On each sheet the 'family' of fractions for each row is indicated under the 0.

Label as many points as possible with fractions as shown in the above diagram.

# Lesson 2  It's a factor

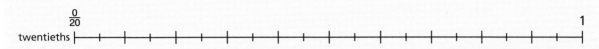

The 20-part number line above can be used to show these 'families' of fractions:

halves, quarters, fifths, tenths and twentieths.

The factors of 20 are: 1, 2, 4, 5, 10, 20.

The 'families' of fractions that can be shown on the 20-part number line have denominators which are factors of 20.

## Activity

Your teacher will give you sheet **2.1**. Label the families for $\frac{1}{2}$, $\frac{1}{4}$, $\frac{1}{5}$, $\frac{1}{10}$ and $\frac{1}{20}$ between 0 and 1 when the line is divided into 100 parts.

## Challenge

On your worksheet, label all the other 'families' shown.

## Lesson 3  Equivalent fractions

$$\frac{1}{2} = \frac{2}{4} = \frac{3}{6} = \dots$$

Since these fractions are equal, they are called **equivalent fractions**.
To find fractions which are equivalent to a given fraction, multiply or divide the numerator and denominator by the same amount.

$$\overset{\times 3}{\underset{\times 3}{\frac{2}{5} = \frac{6}{15}}} \qquad \overset{\times 4}{\underset{\times 4}{\frac{2}{5} = \frac{8}{20}}} \qquad \overset{\div 3}{\underset{\div 3}{\frac{2}{5} = \frac{6}{15}}} \qquad \overset{\div 4}{\underset{\div 4}{\frac{2}{5} = \frac{8}{20}}}$$

$$\frac{2}{5} = \frac{6}{15} = \frac{8}{20}$$

This means that $\frac{2}{5}$ is equivalent to $\frac{6}{15}$ and $\frac{8}{20}$ and also that $\frac{6}{15}$ is equivalent to $\frac{8}{20}$.

It is easier to compare fractions when the denominators are the same, e.g. $\frac{1}{3} < \frac{2}{3}$.

If the denominators are different, convert each into an equivalent fraction with the same denominator.

Example: Is $\frac{2}{5} < \frac{1}{2}$?

A common multiple of the denominators 5 and 2 is 10.

$$\frac{2}{5} \times 2 = \frac{4}{10} \text{ and } \frac{1}{2} \times 5 = \frac{5}{10}$$

$$\frac{4}{10} < \frac{5}{10} \text{ and so } \frac{2}{5} < \frac{1}{2}$$

## Activity

1.  Work through sheet **3.1**.

2.  Write the next four equivalent fractions.

    a. $\frac{1}{4} =$ ☐ $=$ ☐ $=$ ☐ $=$ ☐          b. $\frac{3}{10} =$ ☐ $=$ ☐ $=$ ☐ $=$ ☐

**3.** Find the missing numbers.

a. $\frac{1}{2} = \frac{\phantom{0}}{4}$

b. $\frac{1}{2} = \frac{5}{\phantom{0}}$

c. $\frac{1}{2} = \frac{\phantom{0}}{20}$

d. $\frac{1}{5} = \frac{\phantom{0}}{10}$

e. $\frac{1}{5} = \frac{\phantom{0}}{20}$

f. $\frac{1}{5} = \frac{\phantom{0}}{25}$

g. $\frac{3}{4} = \frac{\phantom{0}}{20}$

h. $\frac{3}{4} = \frac{6}{\phantom{0}}$

i. $\frac{3}{4} = \frac{\phantom{0}}{16}$

**4.** Write down whether each statement is true or false.

a. $\frac{1}{2} < \frac{3}{4}$

b. $\frac{1}{2} > \frac{1}{5}$

c. $\frac{1}{2} + \frac{1}{4} = \frac{3}{4}$

d. $\frac{3}{10} > \frac{1}{5}$

e. $\frac{1}{4} < \frac{1}{5}$

| < | smaller than |
| > | greater than |

**5.** Place two fraction strips end to end on a 'zero to one' line.
a. Write where they end. Example: $\frac{1}{10}$ next to $\frac{1}{20}$ ends at $\frac{3}{20}$. The sum is $\frac{1}{10} + \frac{1}{20} = \frac{3}{20}$ .
b. Find pairs of fractions that end before $\frac{1}{2}$. Write the 'sums' for each pair.

## Challenge

Do the following exercises, if possible, without the 'zero to one' number line.
If you have to look at the number line put an 'L' beside the question and ask your teacher for help if necessary.

**6.** Write the next four equivalent fractions.

a. $\frac{1}{3} = \phantom{00} = \phantom{00} = \phantom{00} = \phantom{00}$

b. $\frac{3}{4} = \phantom{00} = \phantom{00} = \phantom{00} = \phantom{00}$

c. $\frac{5}{8} = \phantom{00} = \phantom{00} = \phantom{00} = \phantom{00}$

d. $\frac{9}{10} = \phantom{00} = \phantom{00} = \phantom{00} = \phantom{00}$

**7.** Write these out in full, putting in the missing fractions.

a. $\phantom{0} = \frac{6}{10} = \frac{\phantom{0}}{15} = \frac{12}{20}$

b. $\phantom{0} = \phantom{0} = \frac{12}{15}$

**8.** Copy and complete these.

a. $\frac{1}{5} = \frac{\phantom{0}}{25}$

b. $\frac{1}{4} = \frac{\phantom{0}}{24}$

c. $\frac{1}{12} = \frac{2}{\phantom{0}}$

d. $\frac{3}{5} = \frac{\phantom{0}}{30}$

e. $\frac{3}{10} = \frac{18}{\phantom{0}}$

f. $\frac{\phantom{0}}{4} = \frac{6}{8}$

g. $\frac{\phantom{0}}{8} = \frac{9}{24}$

h. $\frac{9}{\phantom{0}} = \frac{81}{90}$

**9.** Write down whether each statement is true or false.

a. $\frac{3}{5} > \frac{1}{2}$

b. $\frac{3}{5} < \frac{13}{20}$

c. $\frac{3}{4} > \frac{25}{32}$

d. $\frac{1}{2} + \frac{3}{4} < \frac{6}{8}$

e. $\frac{2}{10} + \frac{5}{10} = \frac{7}{10}$

f. $\frac{1}{5} + \frac{3}{5} = \frac{4}{10}$

g. $1 - \frac{7}{10} = \frac{1}{5} + \frac{1}{10}$

# Unit 4
# Coordinates and shapes

## Lesson 1  Name it

The position of A is given by the coordinates (2, 10). The *x*-coordinate is always written first and both coordinates should be enclosed in brackets.

The line drawn through A and B is infinite but the segment of the line from A to B is described as AB.
AC is a **horizontal** line and LP is a **vertical** line. AC and FG are **perpendicular** lines while AB and DC are **parallel** lines.

The acute angle between MH and CH can be named ∠MHC or ∠CHM.

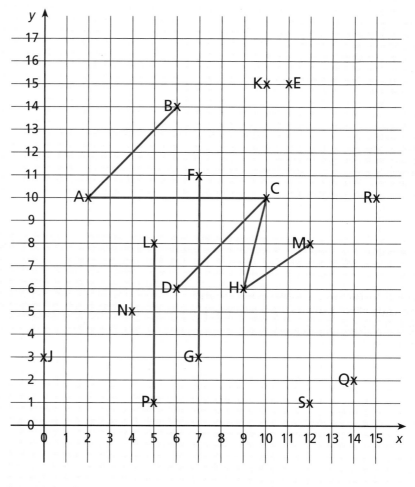

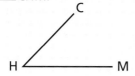

If the **vertex**, H, has only one angle at it, the angle could be named ∠H, although it would have to be made clear whether it was the acute or reflex angle which was being discussed.

When lines are drawn from N to D, D to H, H to G and G to N, a quadrilateral is formed. This quadrilateral is named NDHG.

## Activity

Your teacher will give you sheets **1.4** and **1.7**. Follow the instructions on sheet **1.4**.

## Challenge

Repeat the above activity using sheet **1.5** with sheet **1.4**.

# Lesson 2  What's the point?

## Activity

Play the 'Shape game' with a friend. Copy the axes shown onto squared paper.

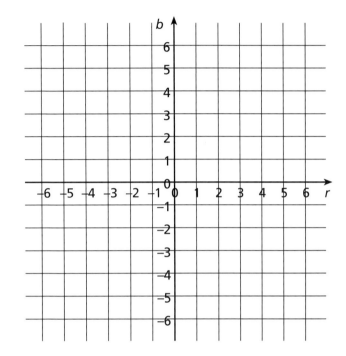

*You will need:*

- squared paper

- a set of shape cards

- two red dice for the numbers on the horizontal axis: one numbered 1 to 6 and one numbered −1 to −6

- two blue dice for the numbers on the vertical axis: one numbered 1 to 6 and one numbered −1 to −6

- a different coloured pencil per person.

Take it in turns to choose one red and one blue dice, roll the dice and mark a point in your own colour.

For example, if you choose:

the positive red dice and roll 4,          the negative blue dice and roll −2,

mark the point (4, −2) in your colour.

Continue until you have each had twenty turns.

Put all the shape cards face up on the table and take turns to choose a shape card.

If you can join your points to make that shape you keep the card.

If you cannot make the shape, put the card back on the table.

*You can only use each point once*

The winner is the person with most cards.

# Unit 4
# Coordinates and shapes

## Lesson 3  Complete it

To complete a square on a grid by marking in the vertex is straightforward

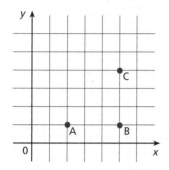

because there is only one possible position to mark.

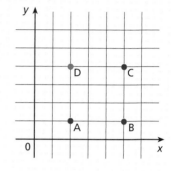

To complete a kite in the same way is more complicated

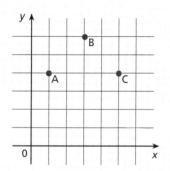

because there are many possible positions to mark.

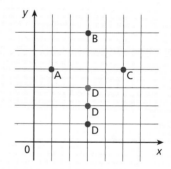

*You will need:*

*squared paper*

Copy the axes shown onto squared paper.

Use the shape cards from the last lesson. Choose a card and draw the shape on your grid.

At the back of your exercise book, write down the name of the shape and the coordinates of all its vertices except one.

Swap your book with your partner to mark the points and find the coordinates of the missing vertex.

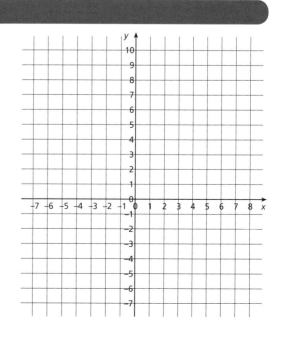

# Unit 5
# In its place

## Lesson 1  Place value

| thousands | hundreds | tens | units | • | tenths | hundredths | thousandths | ten thousandths |
|---|---|---|---|---|---|---|---|---|
|  |  | 3 | 4 | • | 6 | 7 |  |  |
|  | 2 | 6 | 4 | • | 0 | 9 | 1 |  |
|  |  |  |  |  |  |  |  |  |

In the number 34.67:  3 represents 3 tens

4 represents 4 units

6 represents 6 tenths

7 represents 7 hundredths

We can change a fraction into a decimal fraction: $\frac{4}{10} = 0.4$, $\frac{204}{10} = 20.4$, $\frac{6}{100} = 0.06$

We can change a decimal fraction into a fraction: $0.82 = \frac{82}{100}$, $4.3 = \frac{43}{10}$, $4.001 = \frac{4001}{1000}$

## Activity

**1.** Change these fractions into decimal fractions:

a. $\frac{3}{10}$          b. $\frac{23}{10}$          c. $\frac{405}{10}$          d. $\frac{9}{100}$

e. $\frac{15}{1000}$          f. $\frac{607}{10000}$          g. $\frac{907}{100}$          h. $\frac{1100000}{10000}$

**2.** Change these decimal fractions into fractions with an appropriate denominator:

a. 0.19          b. 3.49          c. 20.82          d. 8.1

e. 36.4          f. 0.0038          g. 9.0003

# Unit 6
# Calculations

## Lesson 1  Multiply and multiply

The operations of multiplication and addition are both commutative.

$4 \times 5 = 5 \times 4$   and   $4 + 5 = 5 + 4$

There are usually different methods of working out a calculation but some methods are more efficient than others.

**Examples:**

**1.** $4 \times 18 \times 5 = 4 \times 5 \times 18$

$= 20 \times 18$

$= 2 \times 10 \times 18$

$= 2 \times 180$

$= 360$

**2.** $24 \times 19 = 24 \times (20 - 1)$

$= 24 \times 20 - 24 \times 1$

$= 480 - 24$

$= 456$

**3.** $15 \times 64 = 10 \times 64 + 5 \times 64$

$= 640 + 320$

$= 960$

---

**Activity**

**1.** Work these out in your head.

a. $8 + 8 + 8 + 8 + 8 + 8$

b. $15 + 15 + 15 + 15 + 15$

c. $2 \times 3 \times 4$

d. $2 \times 5 \times 7$

e. $4 \times 5 \times 8$

f. $5 \times 2 \times 15$

g. $5 \times 13 \times 4$

h. $6 \times 23 \times 5$

**2.** Find all the products of three numbers that you can make using three of these numbers.

$$2 \quad 3 \quad 4 \quad 5$$

**3.** Work these out in your head. (You may use jottings if you need to.)

a. $34 \times 10$

b. $42 \times 20$

c. $30 \times 12$

d. $100 \times 17$

e. $33 \times 200$

f. $14 \times 9$

g. $24 \times 9$

h. $54 \times 11$

i. $15 \times 32$

j. $25 \times 16$

Adrone £1.00

Flighter £2.99

Zippy £4.00

Tronic £1.50

**4.** Work out, in your head, how much it would cost to buy the following:

a. 3 Zippys

b. 6 Flighters

c. 15 Tronics

d. 25 Adrones

e. 6 Tronics and 6 Adrones

f. 1 of each type

## Challenge

**5.** Find all the products of three numbers that you can make using three of these numbers.

2   3   5   7   13

**6.** Work these out in your head. (You may use jottings if you need to.)

a. 34 x 20

b. 42 x 19

c. 30 x 17

d. 29 x 17

e. 37 x 9

f. 43 x 99

g. 99 x 68

h. 54 x 101

# Unit 6
# Calculations

## Lesson 2  Dividing up

Division is the **inverse** of multiplication.

If two factors of a number are known, then two division statements are known.

Example:   $45 = 3 \times 15$   so   **a.**  $45 \div 3 = 15$   and   **b.**  $45 \div 15 = 3$

In **a** 3 is the **divisor** and 15 is the **quotient**.    In **b** 15 is the divisor and 3 is the quotient.

Not every division is exact and often there will be a remainder.

The question must be considered carefully before a decision is made about how to deal with a remainder.

Here are some examples of how to deal with $16 \div 5$.

| | **Answers** | |
|---|---|---|
| $16 \div 5$ | 3 remainder 1 | (answer with a remainder) |
| $\frac{1}{5}$ of 16 | $3\frac{1}{5}$ | (answer with a fraction) |
| 16 people go to the station by taxi. A taxi holds 5 people. How many taxis are needed? | 4 taxis | (answer rounded up) |
| 16 pieces of fudge are sold in bags of 5. How many bags can be sold? | 3 bags | (answer rounded down) |
| 5 girls buy a present for a friend. It costs £16. How much does each girl have to pay? | £3.20 | (answer as a decimal) |

### Activity

**1.** Work these out in your head.

   a. $14 \div 7$
   b. Divide 32 by 4
   c. Find one-quarter of 40

   d. Find $\frac{1}{4}$ of 200
   e. Find the value of $\frac{16}{2}$
   f. How many eights are there in 48?

   g. Share 36 stamps amongst 6 stamp collectors.

   h. What is the quotient when 24 is divided by 3?

   i. How many lengths of 9cm can be cut from 45cm?

**2.** Write these out and fill in the gaps.

a. ☐ ÷ 5 = 6

b. ☐ ÷ 3 = 10

c. ☐ ÷ 20 = 4

d. ☐ ÷ 6 = 3

e. 30 ÷ ☐ = 6

**3.** Give your answers to these with a remainder.

a. 19 ÷ 4

b. 17 ÷ 3

c. 13 ÷ 5

d. 61 ÷ 20

**4.** Give your answers to these with a fraction.

a. one-fifth of 23

b. $\frac{1}{4}$ of 13

c. $\frac{1}{3}$ of 20

d. $\frac{26}{5}$

e. $\frac{201}{2}$

**5.** a. Share £50 equally between 2 people.

b. 5 friends share equally a bill of £15.00. How much should each pay?

c. A pack contains 6 small chocolate bars. If the pack costs £1.26, what is the value of 1 chocolate bar?

**6.** Round your answers to these as appropriate.

a. How many four-seater taxis will be needed to take 13 people?

b. How many packs of 4 pencils can be made from 42 pencils?

c. A minibus can take 18 people. How many minibuses will be needed to take 38 people?

d. 24 sandwiches can be made from a loaf of bread. How many loaves will be needed to make 241 sandwiches?

**7.** Make up your own word problems to go with these divisions.

a. 84 ÷ 4

b. 400 ÷ 25

c. 37 ÷ 3

d. £230 ÷ 6

## Challenge

8. Work these out in your head.

    a. 140 ÷ 7

    b. Divide 52 by 4.

    c. Find one-fifth of 110.

    d. Find $\frac{1}{4}$ of 204.

    e. Find the value of $\frac{64}{4}$.

    f. How many eights are there in 168?

    g. Share 360 stamps among 12 stamp collectors.

    h. What is the quotient when 217 is divided by 7?

    i. How many lengths of 18cm can be cut from 72cm?

9. Write these out and fill in the gaps.

    a. ☐ ÷ 5 = 16

    b. ☐ ÷ 3 = 13

    c. ☐ ÷ 20 = 14

    d. ☐ ÷ 6 = 30

    e. 450 ÷ ☐ = 9

10. Give your answers to these with a remainder.

    a. 46 ÷ 4

    b. 57 ÷ 6

    c. 103 ÷ 5

    d. 130 ÷ 20

11. Give your answers to these with a fraction.

    a. one-fifth of 43

    b. $\frac{1}{4}$ of 73

    c. $\frac{201}{4}$

12. a. Share £50 equally among 4 people.

    b. 5 friends share equally a bill of £6.85. How much should each pay?

    c. 7 people are giving equal contributions towards a present costing £22. Suggest how they could do this.

13. Round your answers to these as appropriate.

    a. How many four-seater taxis will be needed to take 22 people?

    b. How many packs of 4 pencils can be made from 142 pencils?

    c. A minibus can take 18 people. How many minibuses will be needed to take 64 people?

    d. 24 sandwiches can be made from a loaf of bread. How many loaves will be needed to make 140 sandwiches?

# Lesson 3  Operating order

| | | |
|---|---|---|
| $(2 + 3) \times 4$ | $2 + (3 \times 4)$ | $2 + 3 \times 4$ |
| $= 20$ | $= 14$ | $= 14$ |

The order of operations is very important. They should be dealt with in the following order:

brackets

↓

division and multiplication

↓

addition and subtraction

Facts to remember:

- the word 'of' is the same as multiplication:  $\frac{2}{3}$ of $7 = \frac{2}{3} \times 7$

- a fraction line means divide and acts as a bracket:  $\frac{28}{9+5} = 28 \div (9 + 5)$

- the order of addition and subtraction can be changed:  $3 - 30 + 40 = 3 + 40 - 30$

- the order of multiplication and division can be changed:  $4 \div 12 \times 36 = 4 \times 36 \div 12$

- addition is associative but subtraction is not:  $4 + (8 + 3) = (4 + 8) + 3$ but $12 - (5 - 4) \neq (12 - 5) - 4$

- multiplication is associative but division is not:  $3 \times (4 \times 5) = (3 \times 4) \times 5$  $40 \div (4 \div 2) \neq (40 \div 4) \div 2$

## Activity

**1.** a.  $3 \times 5 + 2$     b.  $6 + 3 \times 4$     c.  $20 - 4 \times 4$

d.  $(2 + 8) \times 5$     e.  $(20 - 2) \div 9$     f.  $17 - 15 \div 5$

g.  $10 + 3 \times 3$     h.  $15 - 2 \times 6$     i.  $15 \div 3 + 2$

j.  $14 - 10 \div 2$

**2.** a.  $12 - 4 + 9$     b.  $2 - 4 + 9$     c.  $12 - 5 - 4$

d.  $14 - (5 + 3)$     e.  $20 - (8 - 3)$     f.  $8 \times 2 \div 4$

g.  $20 \div 4 \times 2$     h.  $12 \div 4 \times 5$

3. Target

   Using the numbers 2, 3, 4 and 7, find a way to get to each of the following targets. Write your calculation down in one line using correct and efficient notation.

   a. 16

   b. 17

   c. 19

   d. 30

   Now find your own target using only 2, 3, 4 and 7 and see if a friend can work out how to reach it.

4. Some of these pairs are equal and some are not. Write them out, putting in either = (equals) or ≠ (not equals).

   a. 12 – 9 – 2        12 – (9 – 2)

   b. 6 + 7 – 2        6 + (7 – 2)

   c. 3 x 5 + 2        3 x (5 + 2)

   d. 22 – (2 x 8)        (22 – 2) x 8

   e. 15 + 3 ÷ 3        (15 + 3) ÷ 3

   f. (24 ÷ 6) ÷ 2        24 ÷ 6 ÷ 2

5. Some of these calculations are right and some are wrong! Write them out, putting in brackets where necessary to make them correct. Do not change any of the numbers.

   a. 3 + 2 x 2 = 10

   b. 9 – 2 x 4 = 1

   c. 2 x 3 + 2 = 10

   d. 6 ÷ 3 x 2 = 4

   e. 30 ÷ 3 x 2 = 5

   f. 18 – 12 + 5 = 1

   g. 18 – 12 + 5 = 11

   h. 20 ÷ 2 + 3 = 4

6. Copy and complete these calculations.

   a. 3 x ☐ + 2 = 8

   b. 4 + ☐ x 3 = 10

   c. 20 ÷ ☐ – 3 = 1

   d. (☐ + 3) x 6 = 30

   e. ☐ ÷ 3 + 2 = 8

   f. 24 ÷ (☐ + 3) = 6

   g. 6 ☐ 3 x 2 = 0

   h. 15 ☐ (10 – 5) = 3

7. Target with five

   Using the numbers 1, 2, 4, 7 and 8, find as many ways as you can to reach the target 20.

## Challenge

**8.**  a. 3 x 5 + 9

b. 6 + 3 x 8

c. (6 + 8) x 5

d. (40 − 4) ÷ 9

e. 40 − 35 ÷ 5

f. 24 ÷ 4 + 2

g. 30 + 6 ÷ 2

h. 45 ÷ (4 + 5)

**9.**  a. 32 − 4 + 9

b. 2 − 4 + 9

c. 18 − 5 − 4

d. 14 − (5 + 3)

e. 20 − (8 − 3)

f. 8 x 2 ÷ 4

g. 20 ÷ 4 x 8

h. 2 ÷ 4 x 8

i. 40 ÷ 5 ÷ 4

**10. Target**

Using the numbers 2, 3, 4 and 7, find a way to get to each of the following targets. Write your calculation down in one line using correct and efficient notation.

a. 29

b. 18

c. 51

d. 38

**11.** Some of these pairs are equal and some are not. Write them out, putting in either = (equals) or ≠ (not equals).

a. 16 − 9 − 2 ⬚ 16 − (9 − 2)

b. 17 − (2 x 8) ⬚ (17 − 2) x 8

c. (48 ÷ 6) ÷ 2 ⬚ 48 ÷ 6 ÷ 2

**12.** Answer these problems.

a. 45 ÷ 5 + 16 ÷ 8

b. 4 x 9 + 12 − 8 ÷ 4

c. (45 − 30) ÷ (3 +12)

d. 3 + 4 x 7 − 8 x 3

**13.** Some of these calculations are right and some are wrong! Put in brackets where necessary to make them correct. Do not change any of the numbers.

a. 6 + 4 x 2 = 20

b. 19 − 3 x 4 = 7

c. 7 x 3 + 2 = 35

d. 30 ÷ 3 x 2 = 20

e. 38 − 12 + 5 = 21

f. 38 − 12 + 5 = 31

g. 21 ÷ 3 + 4 = 3

**14.** Copy and complete these calculations.

a. 3 x ⬚ + 2 = 23

b. 4 + ⬚ x 6 = 16

c. ( ⬚ + 7) x 6 = 54

d. ⬚ ÷ 3 + 2 = 12

e. 72 ÷ ( ⬚ + 5) = 8

f. 15 ⬚ (12 − 7) = 3

g. 5 ⬚ (9 ⬚ 4) = 25

h. 24 ⬚ 8 ⬚ 3 = 9

i. 8 ⬚ 4 ⬚ 6 = 26

j. 3 ⬚ 7 ⬚ 2 ⬚ 4 = 21

# Unit 6
# Calculations

## Lesson 4  The right column

When adding and subtracting whole numbers or decimals it is important that the place values are correctly lined up.

Examples:  4.82 + 1.49 =  4.82
                              1.49 +
                          ――――――
                              3.33

5.39 – 2.7 = 5.39
                    2.70 –
                ――――――
                    2.69

6 – 1.74 = 6.00
                  1.74 –
             ――――――
                  4.26

## Activity

1.  You can make three pairs of numbers from these three numbers. For each pair find the sum and the difference.    863    504    717

2.  What is the sum of 5618, 4503 and 977?

3.

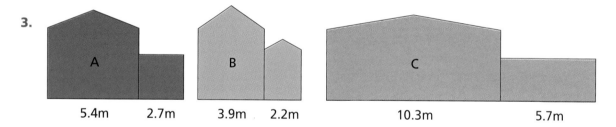

|  | 5.4m | 2.7m | 3.9m | 2.2m | 10.3m | 5.7m |

a.  Find the total width of each house and garage.
b.  How much wider is house A than house B?
c.  Find the difference in width between garage A and garage B.
d.  How much wider is the widest garage than the narrowest garage?
e.  How much wider is house C than house A?

4.

Bubble bliss £4.00          Fantastic foam £2.80          Luxury bathe £4.59

a.  How much more does a bottle of Luxury bathe cost than Fantastic foam?
b.  How much will it cost to buy all 3 bottles?
c.  How much change will you get from £3 if you buy Fantastic foam?
d.  Anna buys Bubble bliss and Fantastic foam. How much change will she get from £10?

5.    a.  5.78 + 0.19          b.  6.09 + 3.64          c.  7.85 – 4.56          d.  4.04 – 3.69

A ———————————————— 3.2m
B ——————————————— 2.75m
C ————————————— 2.4m
D ——————————— 2m
E —————————— 1.8m
F ———————— 1.36m

**6.** The rods shown above come in different lengths. Find the total lengths if rods are put together.

   a. A + B          b. A + E          c. C + D          d. E + F

**7.** For the rods shown above, find the following differences in length.

   a. A – D          b. B – C          c. D – E          d. A – F

**8.** a. 5.7 + 4          b. 6.38 + 4.3          c. 2.85 + 3          d. 2.4 + 7.36
   e. 1.35 + 4.27

**9.** a. 5.7 – 3.5          b. 8.5 – 4          c. 4.75 – 3.4          d. 12.43 – 8.25
   e. 7.55 – 4.8          f. 5 – 2.3          g. 8 – 2.45

**10.** Work out all the additions and subtractions that will give positive answers using any two of these numbers.    4    5.5    5.24    4.6

## Challenge

**11.** You can make three pairs of numbers from these three numbers. For each pair find the sum and the difference.    2863    5046    7517

**12.** You will need to do at least two calculations for each of these.

   a. 7905 – 3718 – 2035                    b. 319 – 184 + 903 – 367
   c. 628 + 547 – (328 – 173)              d. 1000 – 387 + 458

**13.** a. 5.728 + 0.159      b. 6.209 + 3.764      c. 7.385 – 4.654      d. 4.042 – 2.695

**14.** a. 5.7 + 4.4          b. 6.38 + 4.7          c. 1.35 + 2.6 + 4.27      d. 0.475 + 3.04
   e. 2.1 + 3.085 + 5.32    f. 0.009 + 0.999 + 1.001

**15.** a. 5.7 – 3.8          b. 12.4 – 8.25          c. 8.105 – 6.83          d. 4.2 – 1.125
   e. 5 – 0.375

**16.** Work out all the additions and subtractions that will give positive answers using any two of these numbers.    4.375    5.5    5.24    8.6

# Unit 7
# Probability

## Lesson 1  Fair enough?

Decide whether or not the following games are fair.

1.  You need two large counters (or coins).
    Label both sides of one counter with an 'X' and the second counter with 'X' and 'O' respectively.
    One player is 'cross', the other 'nought'.
    Flip the two counters. If two crosses come up then 'X' wins a point, otherwise 'O' wins.
    First player to reach 10 points wins.

2.  You will need three dice.
    The three dice are thrown.
    If their sum is odd, player A wins a point, if not, player B wins a point.
    First player to reach 10 points wins.

3.  You will need a paper bag and four identical counters – two of one colour and two of another.
    Two counters are taken, without looking, from the bag.
    Player A wins a point if the counters are the same colour, but player B wins if they are different.
    First player to reach 10 points wins.

4.  This game needs three counters (or coins). Mark the sides of one with 'X' and 'Y', the second with 'X' and 'Z' and the third with 'Y' and 'Z'.
    The counters are thrown.
    If all three are different player A wins the point, but if any two are the same player B wins.
    First player to reach 10 points wins.

5.  For this game you need a red dice 1–6 and a black dice 1–6.
    Throw the two dice. Make a fraction from the numbers.
    The red dice gives the numerator, the black dice the denominator.
    If this fraction is greater than 1, player A wins a point. If the fraction is less than 1, then player B wins the point.
    First player to reach 10 points wins.

# Lesson 2  Chances

Probability or chance can be measured on a scale from 0–1.

0 ————————————————————————————————————— 1

An event which is certain to happen has a probability of 1.

An event which is impossible has a probability of 0.

Some events have a greater chance of happening than others:

throwing a number less than 5 is more likely than throwing
a number more than 5 using an ordinary dice.

Some events are equally likely to happen:

the chance of a coin showing a 'head' is the same as a coin
showing a 'tail'.

The probability of an event is calculated using this formula:

$$\text{Probability of an event} = \frac{\text{number of ways the event can happen}}{\text{total number of possible outcomes}}$$

When a coin is tossed, the probability of obtaining a head is $\frac{1}{2}$ or 0.5 or 50%.

## Activity

1.  **Letters**

    The letters of the word 'theatre' are arranged on separate cards. They are all turned over and shuffled around. One of them is picked up at random.

    a.  What is the probability that the card shows the letter 'r'?

    b.  What is the probability that it shows the letter 't'?

2.  **Months**

    Each month of the year is written on a card and the cards are put in a bag.
    One card is selected.

    a.  What is the probability that the card shows a month ending in the letter 'y'?

    b.  What is the probability that the card shows a month ending in the letter 'r'?

    c.  What is the probability that the card shows a month ending in the letter 's'?

## Challenge

3.  **Beads**

    A bag contains beads in two colours.
    There are six purple beads and four green beads.
    One bead is picked at random.

    a.  What is the probability that the bead picked is green?

    b.  What is the probability that the bead picked is purple?

    Another bag has fewer beads in it, but the probability of picking a green bead is the same.

    c.  How many of each colour bead could be in this second bag?

    A third bag has more beads in it than the first, but again the probability of picking a green bead is the same.

    d.  How many of each colour of bead could be in the bag? Any other possibilities?

# Lesson 3  Problem solving

## Activity

A group of pupils were set this question. Their solutions are shown below.

Here is a game for two players. Each player has a six-sided dice.

Player A's dice is labelled 7, 7, 7, 7, 1 and 1.

Player B's dice is labelled 6, 6, 5, 5, 4 and 4.

Each player throws the dice. The highest number wins.

Is the game fair? Explain your reasons.

**Ben**
No it's not.

**Jasmine**
It's fair because both have an equal chance of getting a good score.

**Jezz**
Player A will win most of the time because player A's dice has a lot more numbers.

**Amy**
Player B will win more of the time because they have numbers that are all bigger than the smallest number player A has, but they also have 7 which is bigger.

**James**
Player A will win if they throw a 7, but will lose if they get a 1. A has a lot more sevens than B so A will win most of the time. It is not a fair game.

**Neta**
Player A will win with a probability of $\frac{2}{6}$, which is not what it should be, so the answer is no.

**Callum**
Player A's numbers add to 30 and B's add to 30 so it's fair.

Comment on each pupil's response and explain if you think the response is right, wrong or unsatisfactory.

## Lesson 1  Chicken farm

The perimeter of a shape is the distance all the way round it.

The perimeter of this chicken run is 3m + 5m + 3m + 5m = 16 metres.

The area of the chicken run (rectangle) is 3m x 5m = 15 square metres (m²).

Chicken run

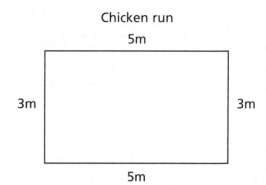

Two shapes can have the same area but different perimeters.

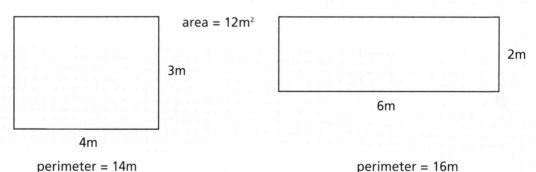

Two shapes can have the same perimeter but different areas.

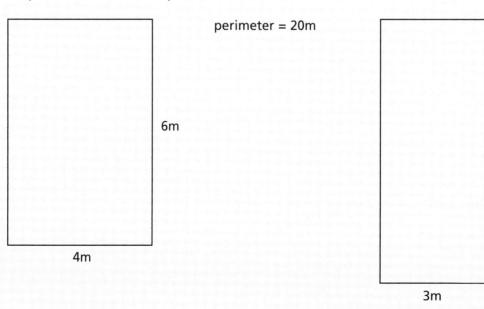

## Activity

1. The chicken run shown in the diagram is in the shape of an equilateral triangle.

   Its perimeter is 21m. What is the length of each side of the triangle?

   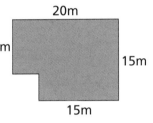

2. Find the area of this rectangular chicken run.

   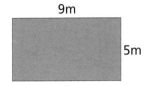

   9m

   5m

   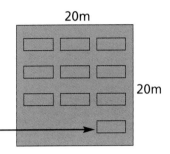

   20m

   20m

3. Find the area of grass remaining in the field (20m by 20m) if 10 chicken huts are placed there, each measuring 5m by 2m.

   Each rectangle is a hut, 5m by 2m.

   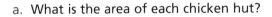

4. a. Find the area of the field shown here.

   b. Then find the perimeter.

   20m

   10m

   15m

   15m

5. The area of this chicken run is 6m² and the length of the shorter side is 2m. What is its perimeter?

   2m

6. Draw another three shapes, each with an area of 6m², but different from the shape in question 5.

## Challenge

7. Four chicken huts (shaded on the diagram) are placed corner to corner as shown.
   The whole area is surrounded by fencing.
   Each chicken hut measures 6m by 8m.
   The perimeter of the whole area is 68m.
   perimeter?

   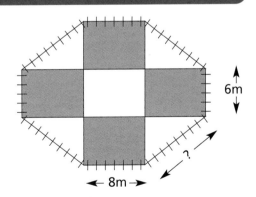

   6m

   ?

   ← 8m →

   a. What is the area of each chicken hut?

   b. What is the length of the edge marked with a question mark?

   c. Is this arrangement possible in a square field 20m by 20m?

8. Investigate shapes for chicken runs that you could make using 24m of perimeter fencing. Which of your shapes has the largest area?

# Unit 8
# Chicken runs

## Lesson 2  Chickens

1.  Using the information given below, design a plan for a chicken farm on a plot of land which is 20m x 20m. Work out how much your plan will cost and how many chickens you can keep.

**Plot of land available: 20m by 20m**

| Costs | | |
|---|---|---|
| Fencing – chicken wire, £2 per metre | Young chick | 100g |
| Fencing posts – needed every 3m, £4 each | Laying hen | 1kg |
| Chicken sheds – £50 per square metre | Table chicken | 2kg |

**Regulations**
There are standards that have to be met to give birds enough room to move around comfortably. These standards are set by the Department for Environment, Food and Rural Affairs (DEFRA).

**System A (straw yards UK – DEFRA)**
Maximum of 3 adult laying birds per square metre
Birds being raised for laying 10kg per square metre

**System B (deep litter UK – DEFRA)**
Maximum of 7 adult laying birds per square metre
Birds being raised for laying: 17kg per square metre
Table chickens: 35kg per square metre

**System C (cages UK – DEFRA)**
Birds being raised for laying: 250cm² per kg

**System D (organic – British Columbia)**
Birds under 3 weeks: 0.05m² per bird
Birds over 3 weeks up to 14 weeks: 0.15m² per bird
Birds over 14 weeks: 0.15–0.2m² per bird

**System E (range hens – four times as much room outside on grass as inside the hut)**
Laying hens: 7 birds per square metre inside
Large chickens: 6 birds per square metre inside
Bantam hens: 9 birds per square metre inside.

# Unit 9
# Written calculations

## Lesson 1 Multiply

There are many different ways to multiply two numbers together.

These activities will give you practice in using some of them.

### Activity

Here are three ways of multiplying 748 by 16. Look at how each is done.

**Method 1.**

| x | 700 | 40 | 8 | |
|---|---|---|---|---|
| 10 | 7000 | 400 | 80 | |
| 6 | 4200 | 240 | 48 | |
| | 11200 | 640 | 128 | Total = 11968 |

**Method 2.**

$$\begin{array}{r} 748 \\ \times\ \ 16 \\ \hline 4488 \\ 7480 \\ \hline 11968 \end{array}$$

**Method 3.**

748 x 16 = 748 x 2 x 8 = 1496 x 8 = 11 968

Which method do you like best?

Can **Method 3** always be used for multiplying large numbers together?

Use the method you are happiest with to work out the answers to these questions.

**1.** a. 253 x 25 b. 523 x 32

**2.** My income is £324 per week. How much is that per year?

3.  How many hours are there in a year?

4.  A cargo ship has 345 containers. Each container has 48 fridges. How many fridges does the ship carry?

5.  Find the missing digits that make this multiplication correct.

```
        5 4 9
    x     Δ 8
    ─────────
      Δ Δ Δ Δ
    Δ Δ Δ Δ Δ
    ─────────
    2 0 8 6 2
```

## Challenge

Use the method you are happiest with to work out the answers to these questions.

6.  a.  138 x 26

    b.  714 x 3.5

7.  How many soldiers are there in 12 regiments if each regiment has 9 companies of 95 soldiers?

8.  Use each of the digits 2, 3, 4, 5 and 6 only once to make two numbers. What is the largest product you can make? What is the smallest product?

9.  Find the missing digits that make this multiplication correct.

```
        4 Δ 3
    x     Δ 4
    ─────────
      1 8 9 2
      9 Δ 6 0
    ─────────
    Δ 1 3 5 2
```

# Lesson 2  Divide

There are many different ways to divide two numbers.

These activities will give you practice in using some of them.

## Activity

Here are two ways of dividing 378 by 24. Look at how each is done.

**Method A.**  $378 \div 24 = 378 \div 2 \div 12 = 189 \div 12 = (120 \div 12) + (69 \div 12) = 10 + 5.75 = 15.75$

**Method B.**

```
        378
      − 240   (10) 138
      − 120   (15)
        18
```

Answer  15 R 18

Can **Method A** always be used for dividing by large numbers?

Use the method you are happier with to work out the answers to these questions.

**1.**  a.  $463 \div 14$ 　　　　　　　　 b.  $975 \div 22$

**2.**  Divide £6725 equally among 25 pupils.

**3.**  How many 5p pieces can you get from £43.05?

## Challenge

Here is another method of dividing 378 by 24.

**Method C.**

```
          1 5 R 18
    24 37¹³8
```

Use the method you are happiest with to work out the answers to these questions.

**4.**  a.  $746 \div 18$ 　　　　　　　　 b.  $486 \div 35$

**5.**  One builder can build a wall in 378 hours. How long will it take 14 builders working at the same speed?

# Unit 10
# Number puzzles

## Lesson 1  Puzzles

When you are trying to solve a mathematical puzzle, you should work logically, asking yourself which answers are possible. Use all the number facts that you know.
If the puzzle is complicated, break it into simpler steps. Then investigate each step.

### Activity

1.  Find the value of each missing digit in the following multiplication sum.

$$25 \text{ x } \Delta = \Delta \text{ 7 } \Delta$$

2.  Each letter represents a particular digit. Within a sum the same letter stands for the same digit – it might represent a different digit in another sum. There may be more than one answer.

a.
$$A \text{ x } A = B \text{ A}$$

b.
```
    A A
x   A A
  A B A
```

c.
```
    A B
x   A B
  A B B
```

d.
```
    A B
x   A B
  C C B
```

e.
```
    A B
x   A B
  C D B
```

*f.
```
    A B
x   A B
  C B B
```

### Challenge

3.  Find the value of each missing digit in this multiplication sum.

```
      Δ Δ Δ
x       Δ 9
  Δ Δ Δ 4 0
    4 Δ 3 3
  Δ Δ Δ Δ Δ
```

4.  Write down any three-digit number. Make a six-digit number by repeating your three digits, in the same order.
    Does your number divide exactly by 7?
    Does it divide exactly by 11? Does it divide exactly by 13?
    Why?

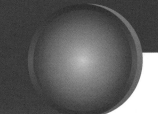

# Unit 11
# Going on and on

## Lesson 1  Sequences

A **sequence** is an ordered list of numbers connected by a rule:

2, 6, 10, 14, …   The rule is 'add 4' to the previous term.

Some sequences involve arrangements of shapes or colours.

To see the rule, look for the pattern.

**Activity**

Your teacher will give you a copy of sheet **1.3**.

## Lesson 2  Patterned or plain?

We can **generate** a sequence if we know the first **term** of the sequence and the rule to calculate the next term. This rule must be clearly stated.

If the first term is 2 and the rule is 'add on 3', this gives the sequence: 2, 5, 8, …

If we know some **consecutive** numbers of a sequence, we can work out the rule.

4, 8, 16, … gives the rule 'multiply by 2'.

If a sequence has a last term it is **finite**:     1, 4, 7, …, 19 is a finite sequence.
If a sequence has no last term it is **infinite**:   1, 4, 7, …  is an infinite sequence.

## Activity

**1.** a. Pamela is making a necklace from white and blue beads. If the beads are numbered consecutively, what sequence of numbers is generated by the positions of the blue beads? Add on the next term.

b. How does the sequence grow from term to term?

**2.** a. The diagram shows the number of chairs that are needed at different sized tables. Write the number sequence and add on the next term.

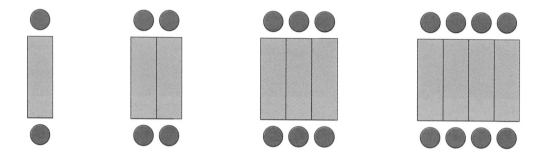

b. How does the sequence grow from term to term?

**3.** a. Copy this pattern and draw the next square in the pattern.

b. Write the number sequence and add on the next term.
c. How does the sequence grow from term to term?

In questions 4 – 10 each sequence shows how many squares or circles are in each diagram.

**4.**   a.  Write the number sequence and add on the next term.

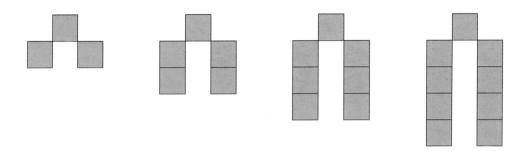

   b.  How does the sequence grow from term to term?

**5.**   a.  Write the number sequence and add on the next term.

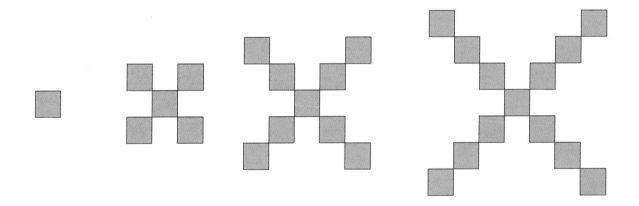

   b.  How does the sequence grow from term to term?

**6.**   a.  Write down the terms of the sequence and continue by adding the next two terms.

   b.  How can the sequence be described?
   c.  How does the sequence grow from term to term?

7.   a. Write down the terms in the sequence and continue by adding the next two terms.

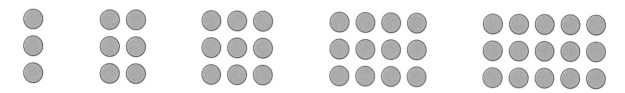

    b. How can the sequence be described?
    c. How does the sequence grow from term to term?

8.   a. Write down the terms in the sequence and continue by adding the next two terms.

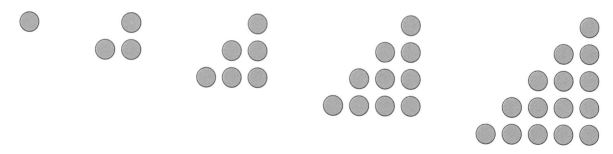

    b. How can the sequence be described?
    c. How does the sequence grow from term to term?

9.   a. Write down the terms in the sequence and continue by adding the next two terms.

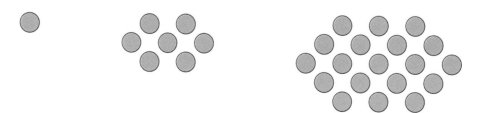

    b. How can the sequence be described?
    c. How does the sequence grow from term to term?

10. a. Write down the terms in the sequence and continue by adding the next four terms.

    b. How can the sequence be described?
    c. How does the sequence grow from term to term?

There are lots of sequences in a multiplication square.

| 1 | 2 | 3 | 4 | 5 | 6 | 7 | 8 | 9 | 10 | 11 | 12 | 13 |
|---|---|---|---|---|---|---|---|---|----|----|----|----|
| 2 | 4 | 6 | 8 | 10 | 12 | 14 | 16 | 18 | 20 | 22 | 24 | 26 |
| 3 | 6 | 9 | 12 | 15 | 18 | 21 | 24 | 27 | 30 | 33 | 36 | 39 |
| 4 | 8 | 12 | 16 | 20 | 24 | 28 | 32 | 36 | 40 | 44 | 48 | 52 |
| 5 | 10 | 15 | 20 | 25 | 30 | 35 | 40 | 45 | 50 | 55 | 60 | 65 |
| 6 | 12 | 18 | 24 | 30 | 36 | 42 | 48 | 54 | 60 | 66 | 72 | 78 |
| 7 | 14 | 21 | 28 | 35 | 42 | 49 | 56 | 63 | 70 | 77 | 84 | 91 |
| 8 | 16 | 24 | 32 | 40 | 48 | 56 | 64 | 72 | 80 | 88 | 96 | 104 |
| 9 | 18 | 27 | 36 | 45 | 54 | 63 | 72 | 81 | 90 | 99 | 108 | 117 |
| 10 | 20 | 30 | 40 | 50 | 60 | 70 | 80 | 90 | 100 | 110 | 120 | 130 |
| 11 | 22 | 33 | 44 | 55 | 66 | 77 | 88 | 99 | 110 | 121 | 132 | 143 |
| 12 | 24 | 36 | 48 | 60 | 72 | 84 | 96 | 108 | 120 | 132 | 144 | 156 |
| 13 | 26 | 39 | 52 | 65 | 78 | 91 | 104 | 117 | 130 | 143 | 156 | 169 |

**11.** a. Look at the column that has the multiples of 9 in it.

   Write down the sequence of numbers in the units column.

   b. What do you notice about this sequence of numbers?

**12.** a. Now look at the sequence of numbers in the tens and hundreds column.

   Write down the numbers in the tens and hundreds column.

   b. What do you notice about this sequence of numbers?

**13.** How can these sequences help with learning the 9 times-table?

**14.** Carry out a similar investigation into the digits in the units, tens and hundreds columns for the 5 times-table.

**15.** Investigate the sequences that can be found in the columns for the other tables.

   Record your results clearly.

## Lesson 3  Is there a pattern?

The rule for finding the next term of a sequence is a number machine.

Feed the number 0 in and the answer (output) is the first term of the sequence. Then feed this number back into the machine to generate the next number.

Continue until the required number of terms is reached.

| Input | Number machine | Output |
|-------|----------------|--------|
| 0 ⟶ | + 2 | ⟶ 2 |
| 2 ⟶ | + 2 | ⟶ 4 |

This number machine has **function** +2. This is called a **term-to-term rule**.

(Some number machines, for example lottery machines, produce lists of numbers that are not sequences.)

### Activity

1. Look at the sequences below. For each sequence:

   • describe the sequence as fully as you can
   • write down the first term
   • write down the term-to-term rule
   • write the next three terms.

   a. 0, 3, 6, 9, 12, 15, ...          b. 15, 10, 5, 0, –5, ...

   c. 7, 11, 15, 19, ...              d. 26, 30, 34, 38, ...

   e. 8, 5, 2, –1, ...               f. 0.5, 2, 3.5, 5, ...

   g. 1, 2, 4, 8, ...                h. 64, 32, 16, ...

   i. 4, 2, 1, $\frac{1}{2}$, ...              j. 1, 1, 2, 3, 5, 8, ...

2. Sequences can be generated by using a graphical (or scientific) calculator.

   To generate a sequence that has a first term of 7 and a term-to-term rule of +5:

   **Step 1:** switch on the calculator and use the calculation mode

   **Step 2:** key in the first term, 7, and press 'enter' or 'EXE'

   **Step 3:** key in '+ 5' and press 'enter' or 'EXE'
   (On some calculators you will need to enter 'Ans +5', but try first without using the 'Ans' button.)

   **Step 4:** press 'enter' or 'EXE' repeatedly to generate the next terms of the sequence:
   12, 17, 22, 27, 32, ...

   > ### *Check your technique!*
   >
   > *Generate the sequence with the first term 2 and term-to-term rule –0.7.*
   > *The calculator should give the terms: 2, 1.3, 0.6, –0.1, –0.8, ...*

Use your calculator to generate the first 10 terms of each of the following sequences, and write them down. State whether the sequence is **ascending** (the terms get bigger) or **descending** (the terms get smaller).

   a. First term 9, term-to-term rule +4.
   b. First term 90, term-to-term rule –5.
   c. First term 120, term-to-term rule –20.
   d. First term 3.4, term-to-term rule +0.4.

Explore the answers to these questions using a graphical calculator.

3. Here is a rule for a sequence: to find the next term add 3. There are many sequences that have this rule. Can you find one for which:
   a. all the numbers are multiples of 3?
   b. all the numbers are odd?
   c. all the numbers are multiples of 9?
   d. none of the numbers is a whole number?

4. Here is a rule for a sequence: to find the next term add 6. There are many sequences that have this rule. Can you find one for which:
   a. all the numbers are odd?
   b. all the numbers are multiples of 3?
   c. all the numbers are odd and multiples of 4?
   d. all the numbers are multiples of both 3 and 4?
   e. all the numbers are multiples of both 2 and 3?

5. Here is a rule for a sequence: to find the next term add 0.5. There are many sequences that have this rule. Can you find one for which:
   a. all the terms are integers?
   b. all the terms are multiples of 5?
   c. all the terms are even?
   d. none of the terms is a whole number?

## Lesson 4  Spreadsheets

The **general term** for a sequence can be expressed as a formula in $n$.

For a sequence whose general term is $5n$:

| | | |
|---|---|---|
| first term | $= 5 \times 1$ | $= 5$ |
| second term | $= 5 \times 2$ | $= 10$ |
| seventh term | $= 5 \times 7$ | $= 35$ |
| hundredth term | $= 5 \times 100$ | $= 500$ |

The term in the $n$th position, i.e. the $n$th term, is $(5 \times n) = 5n$.

This is called a **position-to-term rule**.

It generates the sequence: 5, 10, 15,…, 35,…, 100,  $5n$

Sequences can be generated on a spreadsheet, either by using the first term and the term-to-term rule, or by using the position-to-term rule. You are going to practise both of these methods.

### Practice 1

**Generate a sequence with a first term of 4 and a term-to-term rule of +5.**

- First put in the labels for the rows that will be used. Into cell A1 enter 'Position' and into cell A2 enter 'Term'.

- Enter '1' into cell  B1 since this cell will indicate the first term. Enter '=B1+1' into cell C1 as this will indicate the second term. Enter '=C1+1' into cell D1.

- This sequence has a first term of 4 and a term-to-term rule of +5 so enter the first term of the sequence (4) into cell B2 and then put the rule for getting the next term '=B2+5' into cell C2. Since the sequence grows by adding 5 to get from one term to the next, the rule is to add 5 to the term in the previous cell. As each formula is typed and return is pressed, the value of the next term will be calculated.

Microsoft Excel - Term to term

File  Edit  View  Insert  Format  Tools  Data  Window  Help

Arial    10    **B** *I* U

I2    =  =H2+5

| | A | B | C | D | E | F | G | H | I | J |
|---|---|---|---|---|---|---|---|---|---|---|
| 1 | Position | 1 | 2 | 3 | 4 | 5 | 6 | 7 | 8 | |
| 2 | Term | 4 | 9 | 14 | 19 | 24 | 29 | 34 | 39 | |
| 3 | | | | | | | | | | |
| 4 | | | | | | | | | | |
| 5 | | | | | | | | | | |

## Practice Activity 1

Set up a spreadsheet for each of the following sequences and use it to find the next 10 terms.

Record the sequences.

1.  First term 8, term-to-term rule +3.

2.  First term 200, term-to-term rule −3.

3.  First term 80, term-to-term rule −2.5.

4.  First term 7, term-to-term rule +3.

5.  First term 30, term-to-term rule +3.5.

6.  First term 8, term-to-term rule +0.7.

7.  First term 11, term-to-term rule − $\frac{1}{2}$.

8.  First term 17, term-to-term rule +13.

## Practice 2

Generate a sequence with a first term of 6 and a term-to-term rule of +2.

The process outlined for generating sequences given the first term and the term-to-term rule can be done more quickly by the following method.

- Enter 'Position' into cell A1 and 'Term' into cell A2.

- Enter '1, 2, 3' into cells B1, C1, D1 respectively and click and drag to highlight cells B1, C1, D1.

- Click on the bottom right-hand corner of cell D1 and drag along row 1 to continue to fill in the positions.

- Put the value of the first term, '6', into cell B2 and the formula '=B2+2' into cell C2.

- Click on cell C2 and drag along the row to fill in the values of the sequence.

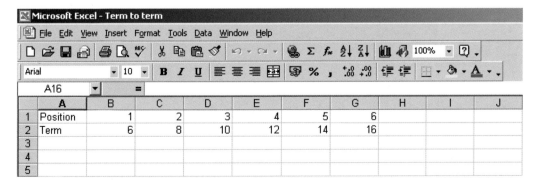

## Practice Activity 2

Set up a spreadsheet for each of the following sequences and use it to find the next 10 terms.

Record the sequences.

1.  First term 7, term-to-term rule +3.

2.  First term 3, term-to-term rule +5.

3.  First term 2002, term-to-term rule −30.

4.  First term 80, term-to-term rule −4.5.

5.  First term 17, term-to-term rule +3.

6.  First term 55, term-to-term rule −5.5.

7.  First term 15, term-to-term rule +3.5.

8.  First term 89, term-to-term rule +0.8.

9.  First term 4, term-to-term rule $-\frac{1}{2}$.

10. First term 27, term-to-term rule +13.

## Practice 3

Sequences can also be generated on a spreadsheet using the position-to-term rule for a sequence. For example, for the sequence with $n$th term $3n + 7$, the first term is 3 multiplied by 1, plus 7, which is 10, and the second term is (3 x 2) + 7, which is 13, and so on.

**To set up the spreadsheet:**

- In cell A1 enter 'Position' and in cell A2 enter 'Term'.

- Into B1, C1, D1, enter '1, 2, 3', respectively.

- Click on cells B1, C1, D1 and drag along the row to fill the cells.

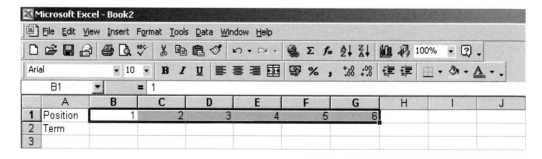

- Into cell B2 enter the $n$th term rule for the sequence ($3n + 7$). Remember that you must enter it in computer language (=3*B1+7). This means 3 is multiplied by the number in cell B1 and then 7 is added.

| | Microsoft Excel - Book2 | | | | | | | | |
|---|---|---|---|---|---|---|---|---|---|
| File Edit View Insert Format Tools Data Window Help | | | | | | | | | |
| Arial   10   B I U   % , | | | | | | | | | |
| SUM   X ✓ = =3*B1+7 | | | | | | | | | |
| | A | B | C | D | E | F | G | H | I | J |
| 1 | Position | 1 | 2 | 3 | 4 | 5 | 6 | 7 | | |
| 2 | Term | =3*B1+7 | | | | | | | | |
| 3 | | | | | | | | | | |

- Click on cell B2 and drag along the row to generate the terms of the sequence.

| | Microsoft Excel - position to terms | | | | | | | | |
|---|---|---|---|---|---|---|---|---|---|
| File Edit View Insert Format Tools Data Window Help | | | | | | | | | |
| Arial   10   B I U   % , | | | | | | | | | |
| C13   = | | | | | | | | | |
| | A | B | C | D | E | F | G | H | I | J |
| 1 | Position | 1 | 2 | 3 | 4 | 5 | 6 | 7 | 8 | |
| 2 | Term | 10 | 13 | 16 | 19 | 22 | 25 | 28 | 31 | |
| 3 | | | | | | | | | | |

## Activity

Following the position-to-term method given in **Practice 3**, set up spreadsheets to generate the first 10 terms of the following sequences. List the terms and say what the term-to-term rule is.

1. $5n + 1$
2. $7n + 6$
3. $7n - 5$
4. $6 + 2n$

5. $3 + 9n$
6. $8n + 5$
7. $10n + 1$
8. $4n + 7$

9. $50 + 9n$
10. $100 + 10n$

## Challenge

Using the position-to-term method, set up spreadsheets to generate the first 10 terms of the following sequences. List the terms and say what the term-to-term rule is.

11. $6 + 7n$
12. $12 - n$
13. $60 - 2n$
14. $3 + 0.5n$

15. $8n - 2$
16. $50 - 9n$
17. $100 - 10n$

# Unit 12
# Just a pile of old bricks?

## Lesson 1  1, 2, 3 bricks

There are three different ways to position a cuboid: standing on its side, on its end, or lying flat.

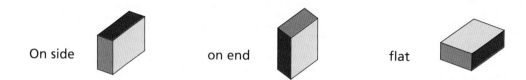

On side          on end          flat

The cuboid can also be seen from two different perspectives: it can be viewed from high up or from low down.

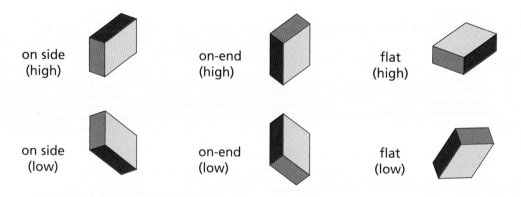

on side (high)          on-end (high)          flat (high)

on side (low)          on-end (low)          flat (low)

You can join two or more cuboids together to form other cuboids, which can also be positioned and viewed in different ways.

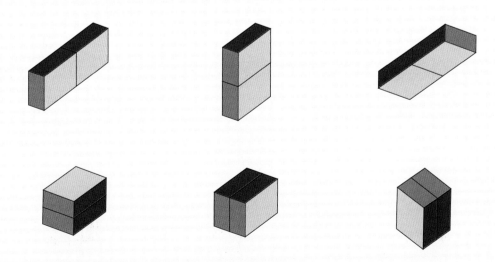

## Activity

> **You will need:**
> two 1 by 2 by 3 bricks made from interlocking cubes, isometric paper

**1.** Using isometric paper, practise drawing a 1 by 2 by 3 cuboid in different ways.

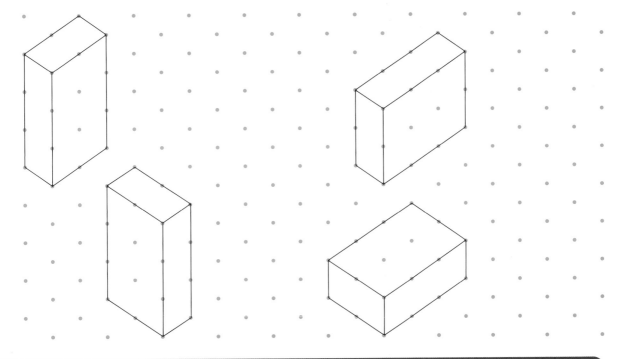

## Challenge

**2.** Using isometric paper, practise drawing cuboids made from two 1 by 2 by 3 bricks.

There are nine possible drawings viewed from above – two have been drawn for you.

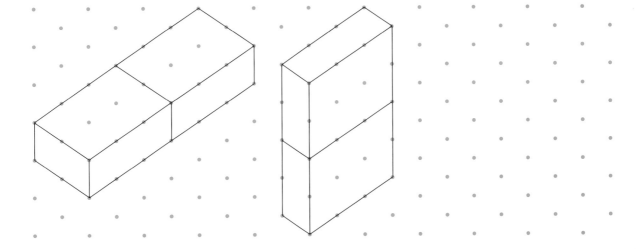

# Unit 12
# Just a pile of old bricks?

## Lesson 2  Surface area

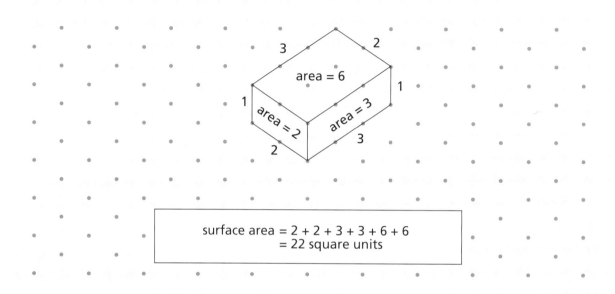

surface area = 2 + 2 + 3 + 3 + 6 + 6
= 22 square units

*You will need:*

*two 1 by 2 by 3 bricks made from interlocking cubes, isometric paper*

**1.** On isometric paper, draw several two-brick shapes and calculate the surface area of each.

**2.** a. What is the smallest possible surface area of a two-brick shape made by fitting together corners of two 1 x 2 x 3 bricks?

b. What is the largest possible surface area of a two-brick shape made by fitting together corners of two 1 x 2 x 3 bricks?

# Lesson 3  Equivalent VIII

Sculpture *Equivalent VIII* by Carl Andre

It is straightforward to calculate the number of bricks in the sculpture shown above.
There are 2 x 6 x 10 = 120 bricks.

If you want to find all the possible cuboid arrangements of 120 bricks, it is much more
difficult. You have to be systematic so that all arrangements are found and none is counted
twice. There are in fact 270 possible cuboid arrangements of 120 bricks.

Consider a simpler sculpture of eight bricks. There are two sets of three factors of 8:
1 x 1 x 8 and 1 x 2 x 4. So there are two different sets of dimensions possible for a cuboid
made from 8 bricks. However, each of these sets will have different arrangements, and each
of these arrangements can be positioned in three different ways (orientations).

## Activity

You will need:

*interlocking cubes, isometric paper*

**1.**  a. Investigate systematically all the ways of arranging four bricks to make a cuboid.
    b. Sketch them on isometric paper.

## Challenge

**2.**  Investigate the surface areas and volumes of all the four-brick cuboids you found in
    the activity.

## Lesson 1  Thirds

When one whole is divided into three equal parts, each of these parts is called a third. This is written as a **fraction** $\frac{1}{3}$, which means one part out of three.

If you multiply the numerator and denominator of a fraction by the same number, you get an **equivalent fraction**.

Similarly, if you divide the numerator and denominator by the same number you **simplify** a fraction.

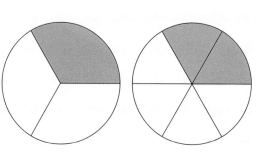

$$\frac{1}{3} \quad = \quad \frac{2}{6} \; = \; \frac{3}{9} \; = \; \cdots \; = \; \frac{7}{21} \quad \text{etc.}$$

$$\frac{3}{9} \quad = \quad \frac{2}{6} \; = \; \frac{1}{3}$$

What fraction of each shape is coloured?

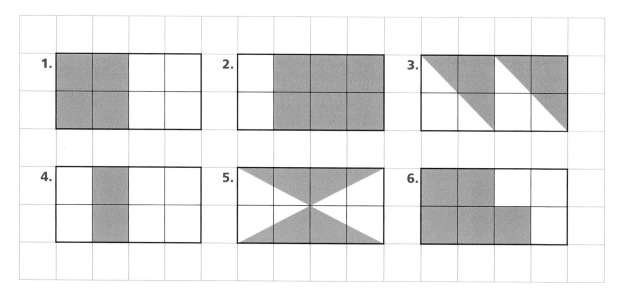

1.

2.

3.

4.

5.

6.

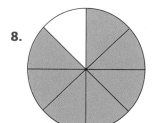

7.

8.

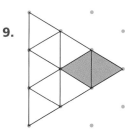

9.

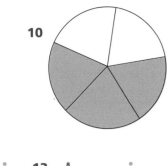

10

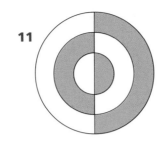

11

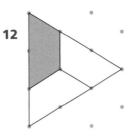

12

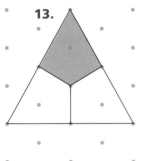

13.

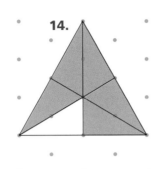

14.

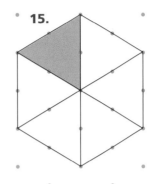

15.

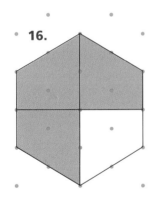

16.

17.

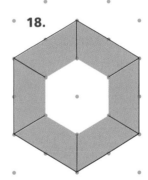

18.

## Challenge

What fraction of each shape is coloured?

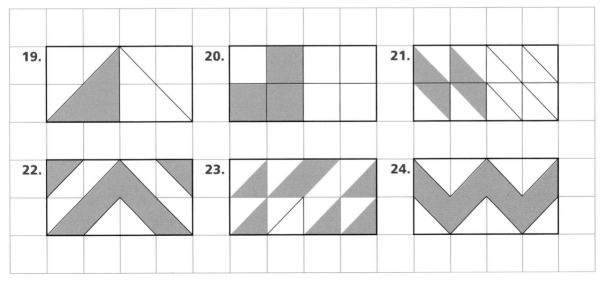

19.  20.  21.

22.  23.  24.

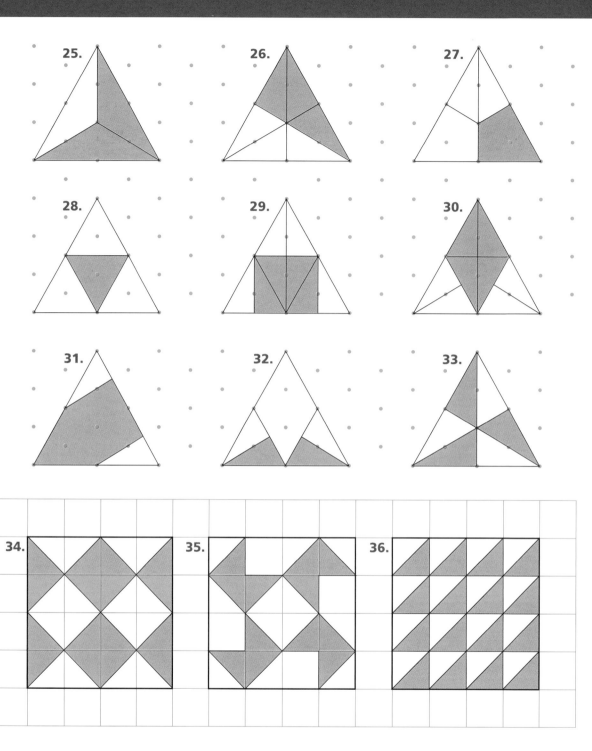

25.

26.

27.

28.

29.

30.

31.

32.

33.

34.

35.

36.

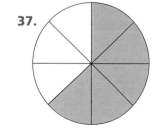

37.

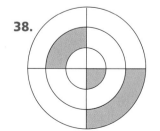

38.

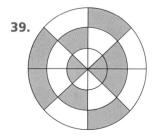

39.

# Lesson 2  Fraction lines

When fractions have the same denominator, it is easy to compare them, i.e. decide which is smaller or larger.

$$\frac{4}{5} \quad > \quad \frac{3}{5} \qquad\qquad \frac{5}{9} \quad < \quad \frac{7}{9}$$

If you want to compare fractions that do not have the same denominator, you can make the denominators the same by using equivalent fractions. You can also compare fractions by using 'fraction lines' as shown below.

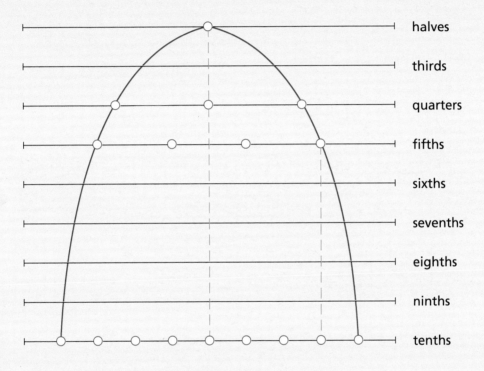

From the fraction lines you can see that:

$$\frac{5}{10} \quad = \quad \frac{2}{4} \qquad\qquad \frac{2}{10} \quad < \quad \frac{2}{5} \qquad\qquad \frac{8}{10} \quad > \quad \frac{3}{5}$$

**Activity**

1.  a.  Copy the diagram below, making each line 12cm long.

    b.  Divide each line into the fractions given and join up the first fractions on each line with a smooth curve.

    c.  Join up the second fractions on each line as a smooth curve, and continue until all the fractions have been joined up.

    d.  What patterns do you see when your diagram is complete?

    |————————————————————————————————————————————————| halves

    |————————————————————————————————————————————————| thirds

    |————————————————————————————————————————————————| quarters

    |————————————————————————————————————————————————| sixths

    |————————————————————————————————————————————————| eighths

    |————————————————————————————————————————————————| ninths

    |————————————————————————————————————————————————| tenths

    |————————————————————————————————————————————————| twelfths

**Challenge**

2.  Can you include the correct positions for fifths, sevenths and elevenths in your diagram for question 1?

# Lesson 3 Comparing fractions

We can write fractions as common fractions or as decimal fractions, and we can change (convert) from one to the other.

| H | T | U | • | t | h | | | | |
|---|---|---|---|---|---|---|---|---|---|
| | | 3 | • | 7 | | = | 3.7 | = | $3\frac{7}{10}$ |
| | | 0 | • | 1 | 9 | = | 0.19 | = | $\frac{19}{100}$ |
| | 1 | 6 | • | 5 | | = | 16.5 | = | $16\frac{5}{10}$ |
| | | 0 | • | 0 | 3 | = | 0.03 | = | $\frac{3}{100}$ |

When you change a decimal to a common fraction, notice that the column heading for the last digit (the one furthest to the right) becomes the denominator.

Remember that fractions can be simplified by dividing the numerator and denominator by the same number.

$$0.6 \quad = \quad \frac{6}{10} \quad = \quad \frac{3}{5}$$

To express a smaller number as a fraction of a larger number, make sure that both numbers are in the same units.

$$40 \text{ minutes as a fraction of 1 hour } = \frac{40}{60} = \frac{2}{3}$$

$$30\text{cm as a fraction of 2m } = \frac{30}{200} = \frac{3}{20}$$

## Activity

1. My flower bed has room for 20 flowers. I plant 12 orange marigolds, 4 blue cornflowers and 4 red salvia. What fraction of the flowers are orange?

2. What fraction of £1 is 10p?

3. A family has travelled 15 minutes out of a journey that takes three-quarters of an hour. What fraction of the journey has been completed?

4. What fraction of a whole turn do you go through in turning clockwise from west to north?

5. Write each of these decimal fractions as a common fraction, and simplify your answer if possible.

   a. 0.3          b. 0.5          c. 0.25          d. 0.7
   e. 0.4          f. 0.09

## Challenge

6. What fraction of a whole turn do you go through in turning clockwise from west to east?

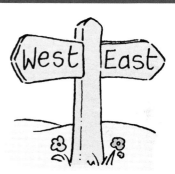

7. A cake needs to be baked for 50 minutes. What fraction of this time has passed after half an hour? Is the cake three-quarters cooked by then?

8. Jen sprains her ankle after running 800m of a 1000m race. What fraction of the whole race did she run? Did she complete three-quarters of the race?

9. Convert these decimals to fractions, simplifying if possible.

   a. 0.18          b. 1.2          c. 1.5          d. 0.61
   e. 0.65          f. 0.6

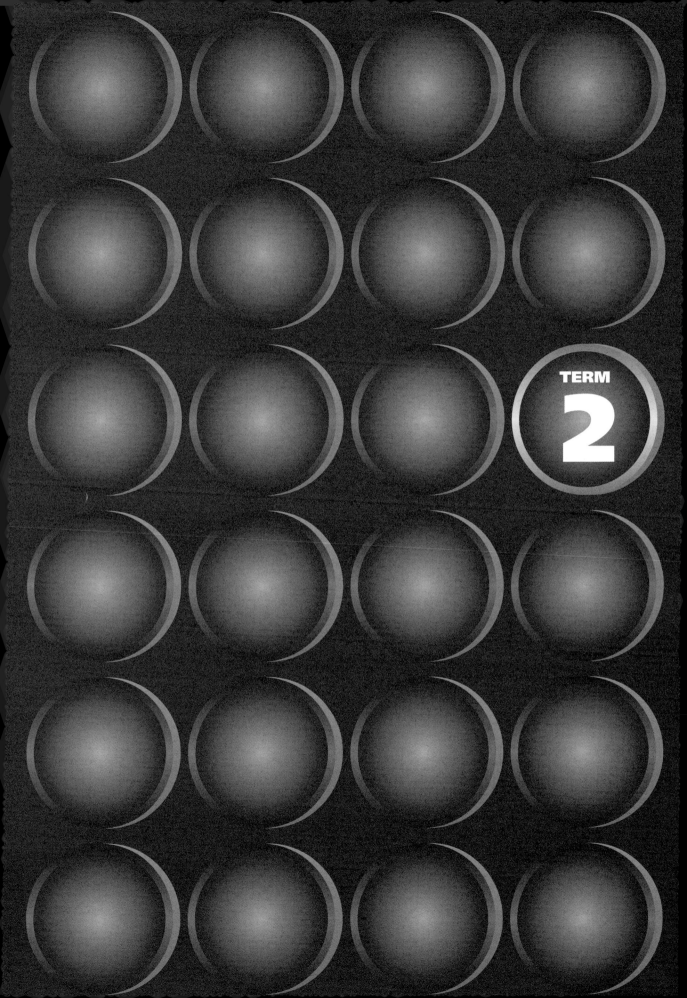

TERM

**2**

## Lesson 1  Constructing stars

A complete turn is 360°.
A quarter turn is 90°.

If 90 divides into 360 four times, then
4 must divide into 360 ninety times.

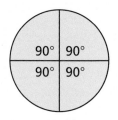

A **factor** is a number that divides exactly into another
number, so 90 and 4 are both factors of 360.

There are many factors of 360.  For example, 10 and 36 are
both factors of 360.

To construct a star:

**1.** Draw a pair of concentric circles.
(Concentric circles have the same centre.)

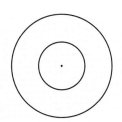

**2.** Choose a factor of 360, for example 36.

**3.** Draw a radius of the outer circle
(a line from the centre to the circumference).

**4.** On the drawn radius, use a protractor to
mark off angles of 36° all the way round
the circle. There will be ten angles altogether.

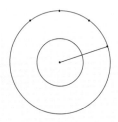

**5.** Draw radials dividing the circles into
ten angles of 36°.

**6.** Construct the star by joining the points
where the radials cross the two circles.

**7.** Ten angles of 36° will produce a
five-pointed star.

Choosing smaller angles will give a star
with more points, and using more than
two concentric circles will produce
more complex stars.

## Activity

> *You will need:*
>
> *pair of compasses, protractor, ruler, sharp pencil, some coloured pencils*

1.  Use the method in the example to construct this star:

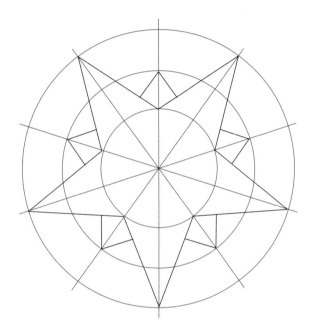

## Challenge

2.  Design and construct your own stars using different sized angles and two concentric circles. The examples below may give you some ideas.

    When you have completed the constructions, colour your stars carefully.

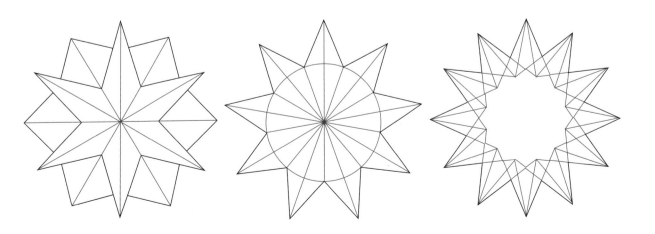

## Lesson 2  Investigating more stars

*Remember:*
*multiples are the answers*
*in the times tables.*

For example, multiples of 6 are 6, 12, 18, 24, 30, 36, 42, 48, 54, 60, …
and multiples of 9 are 9, 18, 27, 36, 45, 54, 63, 72, 81, 90, …

From these lists, the common multiples of 6 and 9 are 18, 36 and 54.

The LCM (lowest common multiple) is 18.

**Star designs**

The design of your star will depend on:

- the number of concentric circles used
- the size of the radii of concentric circles
- the angles between the radials (the chosen factor of 360).

The number of combinations of circles, radii and angles is endless and can produce some complicated and very impressive effects.

## Activity

*You will need:*

*pair of compasses, protractor, ruler, sharp pencil, coloured pencils, squared paper, scissors*

**Special constructions**

Double stars have two sets of radials at different angles.

Spirals can be constructed like this:

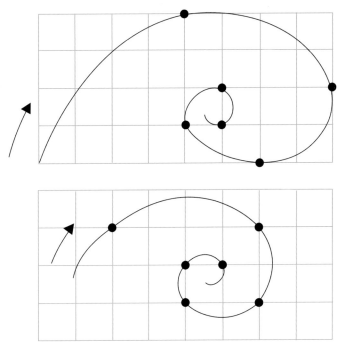

You can cut out the spiral by cutting alongside the spiral line about half a centimetre either side of it.

Stars can be suspended by thread from each dot on the spiral to make a twirling star mobile.

Your teacher will give you a copy of sheet **2.1**.

1.  Construct the double star shown in the example on the opposite page.  Use angles of 45° and 72° to position the radials.

    Colour your star.

2.  Cut out one of the spirals from sheet **2.1** and use it to make a twirling mobile with the stars you have made so far.

## Challenge

3.  Design and construct your own double stars using different pairs of angles.

    Colour your stars and use them to make another twirling mobile with the other spiral from sheet **2.1**.

# Unit 2
# Rods

## Lesson 1  Triangle numbers

The first five triangular numbers are: 1, 3, 6, 10, 15.

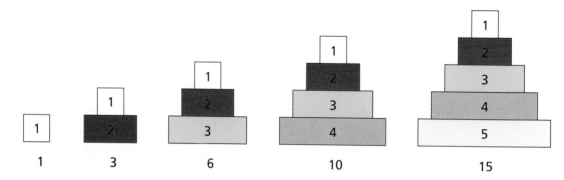

Each new number is obtained by adding on one more than the time before, starting by adding 2 to the first number to give 3 as the second number.

The next five triangular numbers are: 21, 28, 36, 45, 55.

The triangular numbers can also be shown like this:

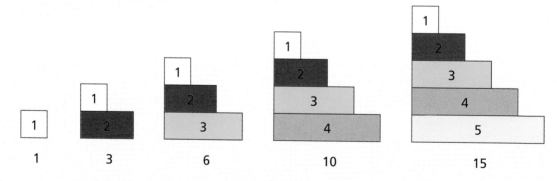

Here, two 'triangles' have been put together to make a square:

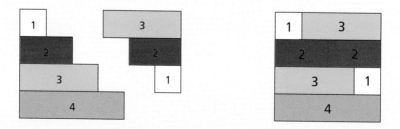

The total of the rods in this square is 16, which is a square number, so that $4^2 = 16$.

## Activity

> *You will need:*
>
> *Cuisenaire rods, or you could make your own from sheet 1.1.*

Use your set of rods to help you answer these questions.

**1.** a. Here are the 'triangles' for the first two triangular numbers:

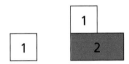

   Put the two 'triangles' together to make a square.

   b. What is the total of the rods in the square?

**2.** a. These are the 'triangles' for the second and third triangular numbers:

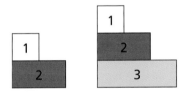

   Put the two 'triangles' together to make a square.

   b. What is the total of the rods in the square?

**3.** Repeat questions 1a and 1b for the third and fourth triangular numbers and the fourth and fifth triangular numbers.

**4.** The totals you found in questions 1, 2 and 3 are special numbers.

   What sort of numbers are they?

## Challenge

**5.** From your work in questions 1 to 4, what can you say about the connection between triangular numbers and square numbers?

   Write your idea as a simple rule that will work with all triangular and square numbers.

## Lesson 2  Multiples

Two 9-rods are the same length as three 6-rods. The length is 18.

$$2 \times 9 = 18$$

$$3 \times 6 = 18$$

**The row length is the lowest common multiple of the two rod lengths.**

Three 10-rods are the same length as five 6-rods.  The row length is 30.

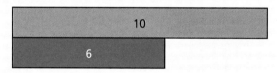

So 30 is the lowest common multiple of 10 and 6.

## Activity

> You will need:
>
> *Cuisenaire rods, or you could make your own from sheet **1.1**.*

**1.** Copy each diagram and complete the bottom row so that it is the same length as the top row. Write down the rod lengths and the row length for each diagram.

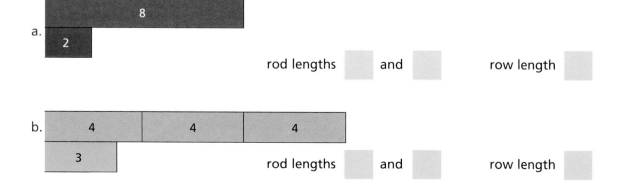

a.

rod lengths ⬜ and ⬜ row length ⬜

b.

rod lengths ⬜ and ⬜ row length ⬜

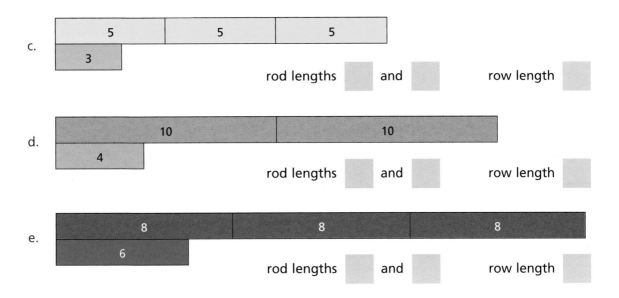

c. rod lengths ☐ and ☐  row length ☐

d. rod lengths ☐ and ☐  row length ☐

e. rod lengths ☐ and ☐  row length ☐

2. Copy each diagram and make both rows the same length in each using the least number of rods possible. Write down the rod lengths and the row length for each diagram.

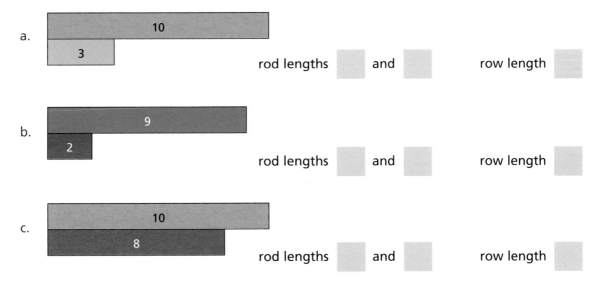

a. rod lengths ☐ and ☐  row length ☐

b. rod lengths ☐ and ☐  row length ☐

c. rod lengths ☐ and ☐  row length ☐

**Challenge**

3. a. Choose some different pairs of rod lengths and find, for each pair, the least number of rods needed in both rows to make them the same length.

 b. Draw diagrams to show the rods you have used in part a.

# Unit 3
# Fractions

## Lesson 1   Working in fours

A fraction has a **numerator** and a **denominator**.

$$\frac{1}{2} \longleftarrow \text{numerator}$$
$$\phantom{\frac{1}{2}} \longleftarrow \text{denominator}$$

In a **proper fraction** the numerator is smaller than the denominator, for example:   $\frac{1}{2}$

In an **improper fraction** the numerator is larger than the denominator, for example:   $\frac{4}{3}$

A **mixed number** has a whole number part and a fraction part, for example:   $1\frac{1}{2}$

**Making fractions**

The numbers 2, 4, 5 and 9 can be used to make these fractions:

$$\frac{2}{2} \qquad \frac{4}{5} \qquad \frac{5}{9} \qquad \frac{9}{4}$$

Use a systematic approach to find all the fractions that can be made from 2, 4, 5 and 9.

$$\frac{2}{2} \quad \frac{2}{4} \quad \frac{2}{5} \quad \frac{2}{9}$$

**2**

$$\frac{4}{2} \quad \frac{4}{4} \quad \frac{4}{5} \quad \frac{4}{9}$$

**4**

**5**

**9**

$$\frac{5}{2} \quad \frac{5}{4} \quad \frac{5}{5} \quad \frac{5}{9}$$

$$\frac{9}{2} \quad \frac{9}{4} \quad \frac{9}{5} \quad \frac{9}{9}$$

To sort a list of fractions into order of size try one or more of these methods:

1.  Sort them into fractions less than 1, fractions equal to 1 and fractions greater than 1.

2.  Separate those less than a half from those greater than a half.

3.  Find a common denominator for the fractions.

4.  Draw simple diagrams to compare fractions, for example:

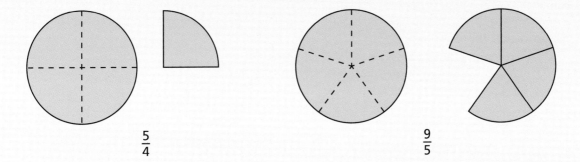

$$\frac{5}{4}$$                                    $$\frac{9}{5}$$

## Activity

1.  Using the numbers 1, 3, 5 and 8:

    a. Write out all the possible fractions that you can make with a numerator of 1.

    b. Write out all the possible fractions that you can make with a denominator of 3.

    c. Write out all the possible fractions that you can make with a denominator of 5.

    d. Write out all the possible fractions that you can make with a denominator of 8.

2.  a. Which four of your fractions are equal to 1?

    b. Which of your fractions are less than 1?

    c. Which of your fractions are greater than 1?

    d. Which of your fractions have the smallest and the largest value?

## Lesson 2  Fraction pizzas

Four children share four different flavours of pizza.

Each pizza is cut into five equal parts or fifths.

In one pizza there are $\frac{5}{5}$.

In four pizzas there will be $\frac{20}{5}$.

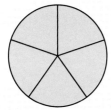 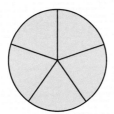 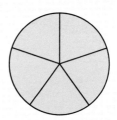 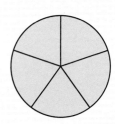

Cheese and tomato    Ham and pineapple    Pepperoni    Mushroom and olive

One child chooses $\frac{2}{5}$ cheese and tomato and $\frac{1}{5}$ ham and pineapple and so has $\frac{2}{5} + \frac{1}{5} = \frac{3}{5}$.

The other three children choose $\frac{5}{5}$, $\frac{6}{5}$ and $\frac{6}{5}$.

Together they have $\frac{3}{5} + \frac{5}{5} + \frac{6}{5} + \frac{6}{5} = \frac{20}{5}$

$$= 4 \text{ pizzas.}$$

If each pizza is cut into eight equal parts:

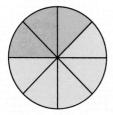 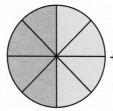 + 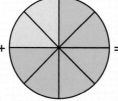 =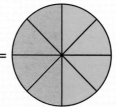

$\quad\quad \frac{1}{4} + \frac{1}{8}$ $\quad\quad\quad\quad\quad\quad \frac{1}{2} + \frac{3}{4}$

$= \frac{2}{8} + \frac{1}{8}$ $\quad\quad\quad\quad\quad = \frac{2}{4} + \frac{3}{4}$

$= \frac{3}{8}$ $\quad\quad\quad\quad\quad\quad\quad = \frac{5}{4} = 1\frac{1}{4}$

## Activity

1. Write down the correct answer for each – there may be more than one.

   a. $\frac{1}{7} + \frac{1}{7}$ $= \frac{2}{14}$ $\frac{1}{14}$ $\frac{2}{7}$ $\frac{1}{7}$ $\frac{1}{49}$

   b. $\frac{2}{3} + \frac{2}{3} + \frac{1}{3} = 1$ $1\frac{1}{3}$ $1\frac{2}{3}$ $2$ $\frac{5}{3}$

   c. $\frac{3}{8} - \frac{1}{8}$ $= \frac{2}{8}$ $\frac{1}{8}$ $\frac{1}{4}$ $\frac{2}{16}$ $\frac{2}{1}$

   d. $1\frac{1}{4} - \frac{1}{2}$ $= \frac{5}{8}$ $\frac{3}{4}$ $1\frac{1}{4}$ $1\frac{1}{2}$ $\frac{4}{8}$

## Challenge

2. Four pizzas are cut up as shown in the diagrams. The cheese and tomato pizza is in quarters, the ham and pineapple pizza is in thirds, the pepperoni pizza is in eighths and the mushroom and olive pizza is in sixths.

   Find the ways in which you can have a total of half a pizza. Record how many slices you can have from each pizza.

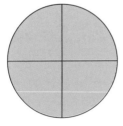

Cheese and tomato

Ham and pineapple

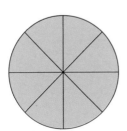

Pepperoni

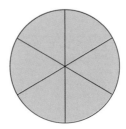

Mushroom and olive

## Lesson 3  More pizzas

Each of these pizzas is cut into five equal parts:

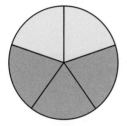  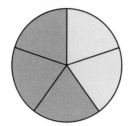  =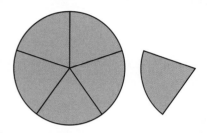

$$2 \times \frac{3}{5} = \frac{6}{5} = 1\frac{1}{5} \quad \text{or} \quad \frac{3}{5} \times 2 = 1\frac{1}{5}$$

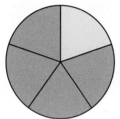  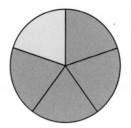  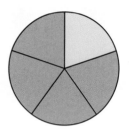

$$3 \times \frac{4}{5} = \frac{12}{5} = 2\frac{2}{5} \quad \text{or} \quad \frac{4}{5} \times 3 = 2\frac{2}{5}$$

## Activity

**1.** Write down the correct answer for each – there may be more than one.

a. $5 \times \frac{3}{4} = $   $\frac{15}{20}$   $\frac{15}{4}$   $15\frac{1}{4}$   $3\frac{3}{4}$   $\frac{3}{4}$

b. $\frac{5}{6} \times 4 = $   $\frac{20}{6}$   $\frac{20}{24}$   $\frac{10}{3}$   $3\frac{1}{3}$   $3\frac{2}{6}$

c. $\frac{2}{3} \times 9 = $   $\frac{18}{3}$   $\frac{18}{27}$   $6$   $\frac{2}{3}$   $1$

**2.** There are three different sorts of mini pizza. Jane takes $\frac{2}{3}$ of each type of pizza. Julia takes $\frac{3}{4}$ of each type of pizza. How much more in total does Julia have than Jane?

pizza 1                    pizza 2                    pizza 3

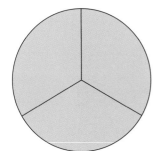   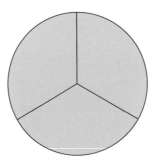   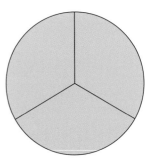

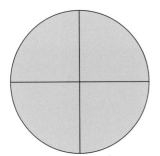   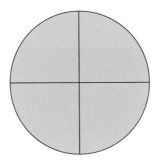   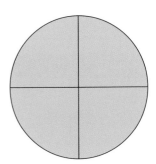

# Unit 4
# Constructions

## Lesson 1   Measures and mensuration

The size of an angle is measured in degrees.

An angle **less than 90°** is **acute**.

An angle **between 90° and 180°** is **obtuse**.

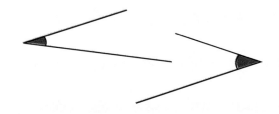

An angle which is **exactly 90°** is a **right angle**.

An angle **between 180° and 360°** is **reflex**.

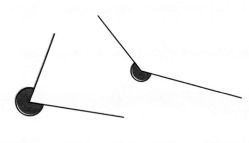

**Take care**

These two angles are the **same size**.
The lengths of the lines (arms) make no
difference to the size of the angles.

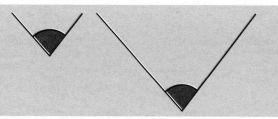

### Activity

*You will need:*

*protractor, ruler*

N

12

**1.**  a. Copy this North line into your exercise book.

Draw lines for South, East and West and add NE, SE, SW and NW
to complete the compass.

b. Copy this line.

Complete the clock face in the same way by drawing lines for each hour.

**2.** a. Estimate the size of each angle below.

b. Measure the actual size of the angles.

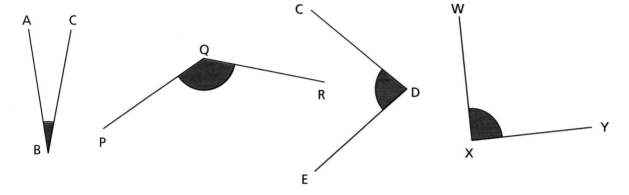

**3.** How can you draw this on a Logo screen?

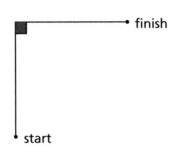

**Challenge**

**4.** a. Draw a line like this in your exercise book:

Find the position of a point C on the diagram, using these clues:

$A\hat{B}C = 70°$

BC = 7cm

b. Can you find another position for C, using the same clues?

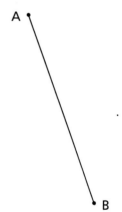

**5.** Why will the following Logo instructions not work to produce this diagram?

FD 20
RT 120
FD 20

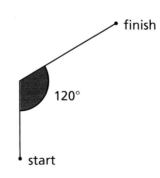

# Unit 4
# Constructions

## Lesson 2 SAS and ASA

Triangles can be constructed when certain information about the sides and angles is known.

**Given two sides and the angle in between**

For example, construct the triangle ABC with AB = 5cm, AC = 7cm and angle BAC = 35°.

1. Draw the line AB, 5cm long.

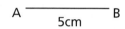

2. Use a protractor to draw an angle of 35° at A, drawing the other arm of the angle 7cm long.

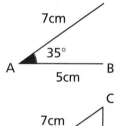

3. Use a ruler to join B and C.

**Given two angles and the side between them**

For example, construct the triangle PQR with angle PQR = 50°, angle QRP = 40° and QR = 8cm.

1. Draw the line QR, 8cm long.

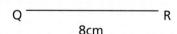

2. Use a protractor to mark an angle of 50° at Q and draw a line longer than it will need to be.

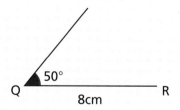

3. Use a protractor to mark an angle of 40° at R and draw the line to reach the line from Q. Label the crossing point P.

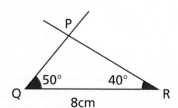

Remember to label the points of the triangle correctly and mark in the given measurements. When the triangle has been constructed, the unknown angles and sides can be measured.

## Activity

> *You will need:*
>
> *protractor, ruler*

**What could go wrong?**

For each of the following sets of clues, either:

draw the triangle, label it clearly and measure any remaining sides and angles, marking these on the diagram with (m) for 'measured'

or

explain why the triangle cannot be constructed.

1. Triangle ABC has AB = 6cm, BC = 5cm and $A\hat{B}C$ = 58°.

2. Triangle FGH has FH = 3cm, FG = 9cm and $G\hat{F}H$ = 135°.

3. Triangle LMN has LM = 10cm, $M\hat{L}N$ = 62° and $L\hat{M}N$ = 34°.

4. Triangle DEF has EF = 8cm, $D\hat{E}F$ = 50° and $E\hat{F}D$ = 140°.

5. Triangle PQR has QR = 4cm, $P\hat{Q}R$ = 120° and $P\hat{R}Q$ = 25°.

## Challenge

6. Some people call triangle descriptions like those in questions 1 and 2 SAS.
   Can you think of a reason for this?

7. Triangle descriptions like those in questions 3 and 5 are sometimes called ASA.
   Can you think of a reason why?

## Lesson 3  What could go wrong?

> **Remember:**
> Triangles can be constructed when we are given:
> * the lengths of two sides and the size of the angle in between them (SAS)
> * the sizes of two angles and the length of the side between them (ASA).

### Activity

> *You will need:*
>
> *protractor, ruler*

**What could go wrong?**

For each of the following sets of clues, either:

draw the triangle, label it clearly and measure any remaining sides and angles, marking these on the diagram with (m)

or

explain why it is not possible to be sure what sizes are intended.

1. Triangle XYZ in which XY = 6cm, $Y\hat{X}Z$ = 120° and $X\hat{Y}Z$ = 30°.

2. Triangle ABC in which AB = 5cm, BC = 12cm and $A\hat{B}C$ = 90°.

3. Triangle STU in which $S\hat{U}T$ = 32°, UT = 8cm and ST = 6cm.

### Challenge

4. Triangle RST in which $R\hat{S}T$ = 60°, $S\hat{R}T$ = 100° and $R\hat{T}S$ = 20°.

5. Triangle FGH in which FH = 7cm, FG = 5cm and $F\hat{H}G$ = 25°.

# Lesson 4 Drawing polygons

**Using Logo**

Move the turtle forward by writing the word followed by a number, for example: FORWARD 100.

Experiment with different sizes until you feel happy about the scale on your computer.

You can abbreviate this instruction to FD 100.

Be careful about spaces – Logo needs the grammar to be correct!

RIGHT 90 means turn right 90° (abbreviated to RT 90).

LEFT 70 means turn left 70° (abbreviated to LT 70).

The repeat instruction saves you time if you want a particular set of instructions to be carried out several times. Try altering the numbers in question 2 to check out how this works.

TO OCTAGON
REPEAT 8 [FD 20 RT 45]
END

The above instruction is an example of a procedure which the computer will remember. When you type in OCTAGON, the shape will be drawn on screen.

## Activity

1. Use Logo to draw an equilateral shape with each corner 90°. What is this shape called?

2. What does this instruction do: REPEAT 6[FD 20 RT 60]?

3. Draw a star shape, using lines that are all the same length and angles of 36° at each point. How many points has this star?

## Challenge

4. Design your own interesting pattern. Make sure that you can remember what instructions you used!

# Unit 5
# Negative numbers

## Lesson 1  In order

This number line could represent a thermometer scale. The temperatures are coldest at the bottom of the scale and warmest at the top of the scale.

For example, –6°C is a lower temperature than –3°C.

So –6°C < –3°C

This can also be written as –3°C > –6°C.

Remember, the two statements above are equivalent.

A number line can help you to work with negative numbers.

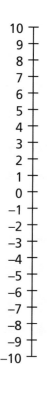

---

### Activity

1.  Work with a partner.

    Take turns to think of two **negative** numbers.

    Challenge your partner to find the number which is halfway between your chosen numbers.

    You may find it helpful to sketch number lines.

---

### Challenge

2.  Continue to work with a partner, taking turns to choose two numbers, but this time only one of your numbers should be negative.

    Again, challenge your partner to find the number which is halfway between your chosen numbers.

# Lesson 2  The joke competition

These number lines show one way to add or subtract using negative numbers.

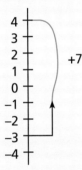

This line shows the sum:

$-3 + 7$

Start at –3 and count up 7 steps to get to 4.

So –3 + 7 = 4

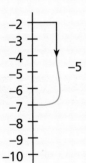

This line shows the sum:

$-2 - 5$

Start at –2 and count down 5 steps to get to –7.

So –2 – 5 = –7

### Adding a negative number

In a game, the scores are –2, 4, –3 and 2. The total of these scores is 1.
Adding a score of –4 to the total gives the new total of:      1 + –4 = –3

> *Adding a negative number has the same effect as subtracting a positive number.*

### Subtracting a negative number

If the scores are 3, –2, 4, –3 and 2, the total is 4.
Removing the score of –3 gives the new total of:      4 – –3 = 7

> *Subtracting a negative number has the same effect as adding a positive number.*

## Activity

1. Copy and complete this addition table by adding the numbers in the top row to the numbers in the left-hand column.

| + | 5 | 4 | 3 | 2 | 1 | 0 | −1 | −2 | −3 | −4 | −5 |
|---|---|---|---|---|---|---|----|----|----|----|----|
| 5 | | | | | | | | | | | |
| 4 | | | | | | | | | | | |
| 3 | | | | | | | | | | | |
| 2 | | | | | | | | | | | |
| 1 | | | | | | | | | | | |
| 0 | | | | | | | | | | | |
| −1 | | | | | | | | | | | |
| −2 | | | | | | | | | | | |
| −3 | | | | | | | | | | | |
| −4 | | | | | | | | | | | |
| −5 | | | | | | | | | | | |

Once you have started, look for patterns which will help you.

## Challenge

2. Copy and complete this subtraction table by subtracting the numbers in the top row from the numbers in the left-hand column.

| − | 5 | 4 | 3 | 2 | 1 | 0 | −1 | −2 | −3 | −4 | −5 |
|---|---|---|---|---|---|---|----|----|----|----|----|
| 5 | | | | | | | | | | | |
| 4 | | | | | | | | | | | |
| 3 | | | | | | | | | | | |
| 2 | | | | | | | | | | | |
| 1 | | | | | | | | | | | |
| 0 | | | | | | | | | | | |
| −1 | | | | | | | | | | | |
| −2 | | | | | | | | | | | |
| −3 | | | | | | | | | | | |
| −4 | | | | | | | | | | | |
| −5 | | | | | | | | | | | |

Again, you should look for patterns to help you complete the table.

# Lesson 3  Puzzles

### Arithmogons

An arithmogon looks like this:

The number in each square is the sum of the numbers in the two circles on either side of it, on the same straight line.

So 2 + 4 = 6,  3 + 2 = 5 and 3 + 4 = 7.

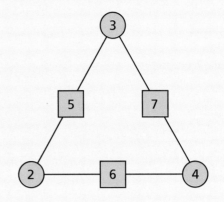

### Number walls

In a number wall, the number on each brick is the sum of the numbers on the two bricks in the row immediately below.

So 2 + 3 = 5,  3 + 6 = 9 and 9 + 5 = 14.

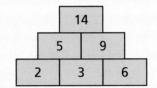

## Activity

You may choose whether to work on arithmogons or number walls.

For arithmogons you will need sheets **3.1** and **3.2** from your teacher.

For number walls you will need sheets **3.3** and **3.4** from your teacher.

**1.** Find the missing numbers in the arithmogons on sheet **3.1**.

or

**1.** Find the missing numbers to complete the walls on sheet **3.3**.

For the Challenge, see page 88.

## Challenge

2.  Use sheet **3.2** to investigate the following question about arithmogons.

    Is it possible for all three numbers in the squares to be 0?

    Give an example or try to explain why it is not possible.

    or

2.  Use sheet **3.4** to investigate the following question about number walls.

    In a 3-layer wall, the three numbers in the bottom row are all the same negative number.

    How is the number at the top related to the number on the bricks on the bottom row?

## Lesson 1  Words or pictures?

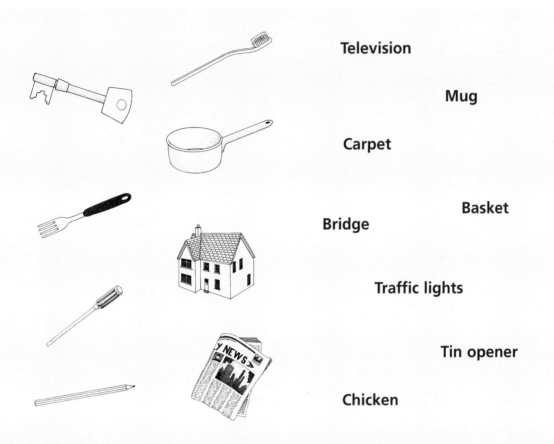

Television

Mug

Carpet

Basket

Bridge

Traffic lights

Tin opener

Chicken

*'People remember a list of objects given as pictures more easily than a list of objects given as words.'*

This statement can be investigated experimentally and the results recorded in a **data collection sheet**.

Example:

| Score | Tally | Frequency | Score x frequency |
|---|---|---|---|
| 2 | ⁤HHt  II | 7 | 14 |

This means that 2 words were remembered by 7 people, so 14 words were remembered.

The completed data is then analysed by drawing charts and finding the **mean**, **mode** and **range**.

The original statement or **hypothesis** can then be proved or disproved.

Your teacher will run the memory test for your class and your class will collect the data.

*Remember:*
The **mean** is found by calculating the total of all the numbers remembered and dividing the total by the number of people taking part.
The **mode** is the number which occurs most frequently in the data.
The **range** is the difference between the largest and the smallest numbers.

## Activity

*You will need:*

*data collected by your class on words and pictures remembered*

1. Draw two separate bar charts for the data on pictures remembered and words remembered.

   Remember to label your diagrams and give each one a title.

2. What is the modal number of objects remembered for each method?

3. Calculate the range for each method.

## Challenge

4. Calculate the mean for each method.

5. Write a short report about your findings.

# Lesson 2  Is everyone the same?

The data collected from the memory tests in Lesson 1 can be used to extend the investigation to test this question:

*Does everyone find it easier*

*to remember pictures than words?*

This can be done by analysing the results for each person and then using a suitable data collection sheet to collect the information about everyone's results.

## Activity

1. Look at your own results from the memory test.
   Did you remember more pictures than words, more words than pictures, or the same number of both?

2. Prepare your own data collection table for recording the class results in the three categories mentioned in question 1.

3. Analyse the data by drawing suitable graphs and diagrams.

## Challenge

4. Write a short report about your findings, using your graphs and diagrams to illustrate it.

## Lesson 3  Memory and age

A lot of data on memory from the previous two lessons is now available.

For a full analysis, this must be pulled together and presented in an appropriate way.

### Activity

1. As a group, collect together **all** your work from the previous two lessons. Organise the data in such a way that you can prepare a display of your findings.

2. Where necessary, find all the appropriate averages and the range, using **all** your sources.

3. As a group, display your work in the form of a poster.

### Challenge

4. Include in your poster a short report which analyses and explains the results of your investigation.

## Lesson 1  Expressions

An **expression** consists of one or more terms.

8 is an expression with one term.

$3n$ is an expression with one term.

$3n + 8$ is an expression with two terms.

8 is a **constant** term because it does not change.

$3n$ is a **variable** term because it depends on the value of $n$.

This pot contains $m$ gold coins.
The number of coins = $m$

**More coins are added.**

The expression for the total number of coins is $m + 2$.

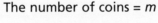

The expression for the total number of coins
= $m + m + 3$
= $2m + 3$

**Some coins have fallen out.**

The expression for the total number of coins is $m - 5$.

The expression for the total number of coins
= $m + m - 3$
= $2m - 3$

## Activity

1. At the end of a rainbow there are 12 pots. Each pot contains the same number of gold coins (*m*). On St Stephen's night, the leprechauns move coins from one pot to another, as the arrows show.

   For each pot, write an expression for the number of coins left after the leprechauns have been at work.

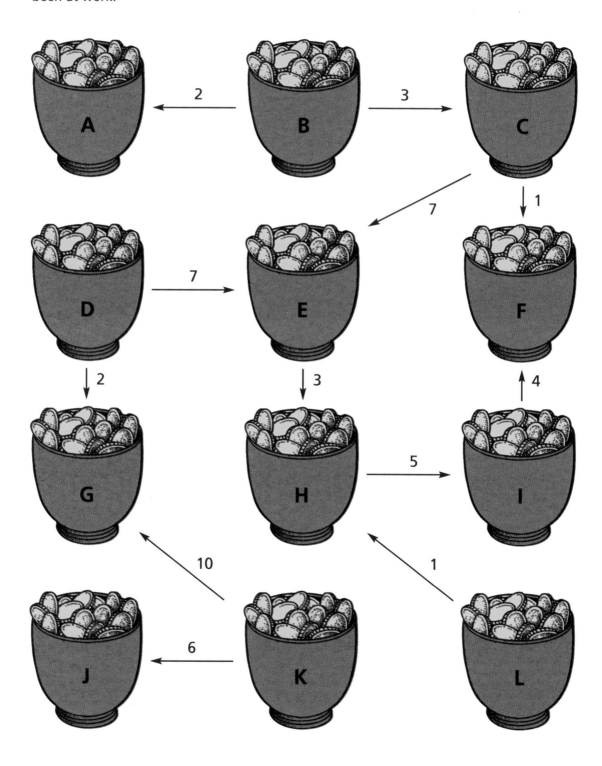

### Challenge

2.  Here are another 12 pots, each with the same number of gold coins (*m*).

    For each pot, write an expression for the number of coins left after the leprechauns have been at work again.

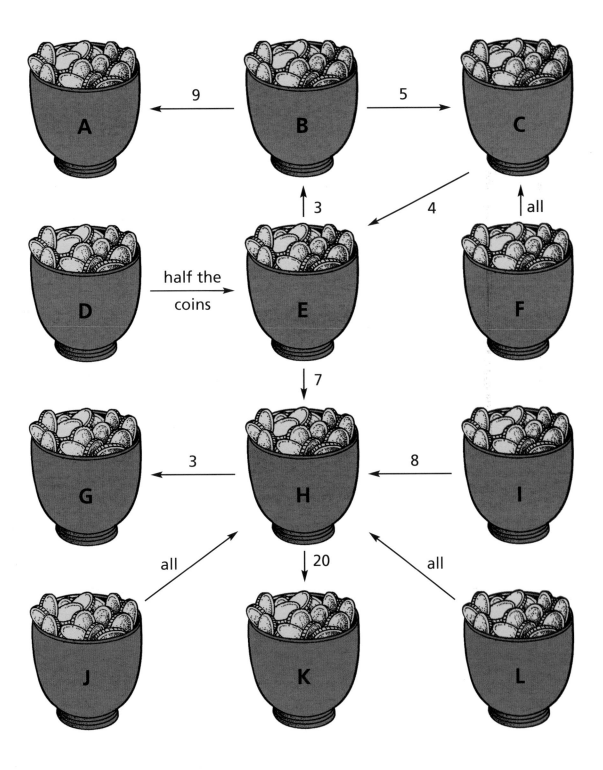

# Unit 7
# Pots of gold

## Lesson 2  Equations

An **equation** is a mathematical statement that one expression is equal to another.

Examples:
$$3m = 6$$
$$m + 9 = 23$$

'*m*' represents a number.

Finding this number is called 'solving the equation'.

The number of coins in the pot is 23.

$$m + 9 = 23$$
$$m = 23 - 9$$
$$m = 14$$

$m + 9$

The solution to the above equation is 14.

In real life, some equations do not have appropriate solutions.

Examples:

$$2m + 1 = 4$$
$$2m = 3$$
$$m = \tfrac{3}{2}$$

$$m + 20 = 15$$
$$m = -5$$

These would not be appropriate for pots of coins because we cannot have fractions of coins or negative numbers of coins.

### Activity

1. On the pots shown opposite, six of the expressions are numbers and six of the expressions consist of two terms, one of which involves a variable *m*.

   a. Use the expressions on the pots to form six equations.

   b. Draw a number machine for each of your equations and solve it to find a value for *m*.

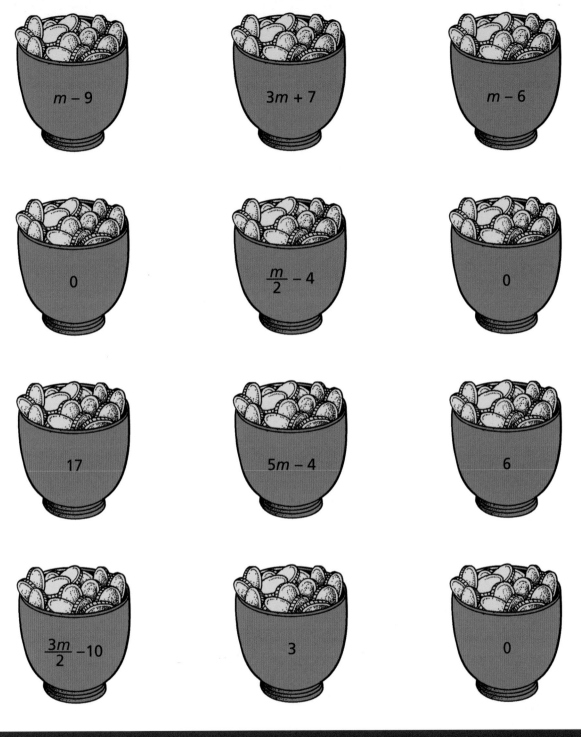

$m - 9$

$3m + 7$

$m - 6$

$0$

$\dfrac{m}{2} - 4$

$0$

$17$

$5m - 4$

$6$

$\dfrac{3m}{2} - 10$

$3$

$0$

**Challenge**

2.  Try to solve the equation $3m + 7 = m + 9$.

    How did you do it?

## Lesson 3  Substituting

The leprechauns are moving coins again!

Three pots contain *k*, 2*k* and 3*k* coins as shown.

Half of the coins in the middle pot are moved to the third pot.

The pots now contain *k*, *k* and 3*k* + *k* coins.

If we know the value of *k*, we can substitute this value into the expression to find out how many coins were in each pot before and after.

Suppose *k* = 12:

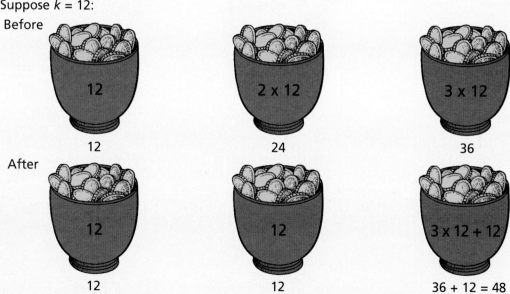

## Activity

1.  The leprechauns have moved more coins:

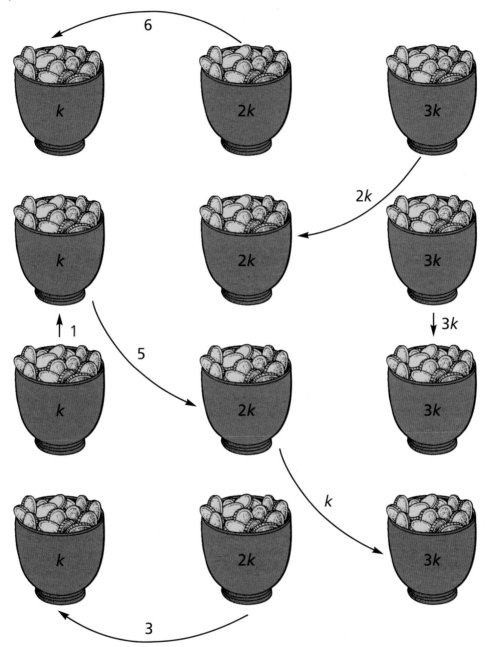

a.  Using the information above, write a new expression for each pot for the number of coins after the moves.

b.  If $k = 10$, use substitution to find the number of coins in each pot.

## Challenge

2.  a.  Make up some moves of your own, and show them on a diagram in your exercise book.

b.  Write down the new expression for each pot.

c.  Find the new total of coins in each pot by substituting $k = 10$ into your expressions.

## Lesson 1  Rough estimates

A weathervane points in four directions. Starting from north and moving in a **clockwise** direction, these are North, East, South and West.

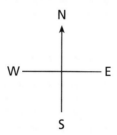

As the weathervane moves in a clockwise direction from North to East, it turns 90°. So the angle between North and East in a clockwise direction is 90°. However, the angle between North and East in an anti-clockwise direction is 270°.

A basic compass will give at least eight directions.

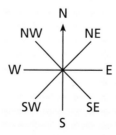

The four additional directions divide each 90° angle into two, giving eight angles of 45°. The angle between North-east and East in a clockwise direction is 45°. The angle between North-west and South in an anti-clockwise direction is 135°.

## Activity

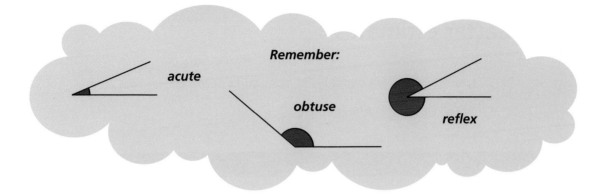

*Remember:*

acute

obtuse

reflex

For each of the weathervanes shown below:

a.   draw a compass sketch to show the wind direction

b.   write down an estimate of the angle between the wind direction and due North

c.   write down whether the angle in part b is acute, obtuse or reflex.

**1.**

**2.**

**3.**

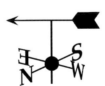

**4.**

## Challenge

**5.**

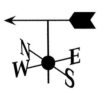

**6.**

**7.**

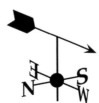

**8.**

# Unit 8
# Weathervanes

## Lesson 2  Better estimates

This activity will help you to improve your skills in estimating angle sizes.

### Activity

> *You will need:*
>
> *scissors, sticky tape*

Your teacher will give you a copy of sheets **2.3**, **2.4** and **2.5**.

- In the instructions below, 'the blank sides' of the pieces in the diagrams are the sides where nothing is printed.

- It is important to position piece A on piece C correctly.

Work in pairs. Follow these instructions to assemble a flying pig angle demonstrator.

1.  From sheet **2.3**, cut out the flying pig and attached strip as one piece (piece A).

2.  From sheet **2.4**, cut out the whole circular piece (piece B). On the blank side, draw a line from the centre of the circle to the edge exactly under the 0° line on the printed side.

3.  Carefully cut out the small black circle from piece B to make a central circular hole.

4.  From sheet **2.5**, cut out the circular piece (piece C). Draw a radius on the blank side, in exactly the same position as the existing one.

5.  Thread the strip on piece A through the hole in piece B from the blank side.

6.  Fold the black part of the strip on piece A so that it is at right-angles to the white piece.

7.  Place the underside of the black part of the strip on the blank side of piece C. The edge between the black and white parts of the strip should lie along the position of the line on piece C, but on the underside. One end of the edge should be at the centre of the circle. Tape over the black part to secure it flat on piece C. With the marked radius on piece C lined up with 0° on piece B, the flying pig should also be pointing in the direction of 0°.

8.  Push piece B down onto piece C.

9.  With pieces B and C flat on the table, the white strip of piece A should be vertical. The flying pig on top of the white strip should resemble a weathervane. You should be able to rotate the flying pig smoothly, so that piece C also rotates while piece B stays still.

**10.** Hold pieces B and C firmly together at the bottom of the white strip and lift up the whole thing so that you can see the printed sides of pieces B and C. As you rotate the flying pig, the line on piece C should rotate round the angle measurer on piece B.

**Using the angle demonstrator:**

- In each pair, one person holds the angle demonstrator with the flying pig pointing towards the other person.

- The first person should line up the printed radius with 0°. The second person will now see the flying pig exactly over the drawn radius on piece B.

- The first person rotates piece C and stops it at an angle which only they can see and read on the scale.

- The second person should estimate the angle through which the flying pig has turned.

- The first person reads the actual angle and writes down the difference between this and the estimate. This is the first person's score.

- The two players then swap roles and repeat the steps above.

- Continue to swap, estimate angles and record scores until the competition is over.

- The person with the highest score wins.

## Lesson 1  Lift journeys

This is Hotel negatif.

It has been built into the side of a hill, with the main entrance in the middle of the hotel, on the ground floor at level zero.

The hotel has ten floors above the ground floor, numbered 1 to 10, and ten floors below the ground floor, numbered −1 to −10.

The control panel in the lift has all the floors numbered from −10, through 0 to 10.

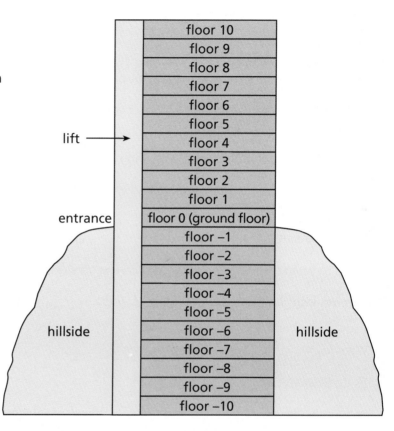

To find how many floors the lift travelled from floor 4 to floor 10, write

(final position) − (starting position) = distance

This gives:    $10 - 4 = 6$

The lift has travelled 6 floors. Since 6 is positive, the lift has gone up 6 floors.

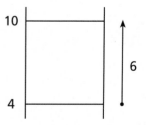

What happens if the lift travels from floor 10 to floor 4?

Final position minus starting position gives:    $4 - 10 = -6$

In this case, the lift has again travelled 6 floors, but since the distance is negative the lift has gone down 6 floors.

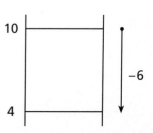

## Activity

Use the drawing of the Hotel negatif to help you answer these questions.

1. For each of the following examples, find:

   - how many floors the lift has travelled through

   - in which direction the lift has travelled.

   a. floor 3 to floor 6

   b. floor –1 to floor 5

   c. floor –8 to floor –2

   d. ground floor to floor 7

   e. floor –4 to ground floor

   f. floor –3 to floor –9


2. You are on floor 2. What is the longest lift journey possible by pressing a lift button only once?

   a. Which floor button would you press?

   b. How many floors would the lift travel? Show your calculation.

   c. Would the lift travel up or down? How do you know this from your calculation?


## Challenge

3. Someone gets into the lift on floor –5. They want to go to the ground floor but, by mistake, they press the button for another floor. When the lift arrives at that floor the person realises their mistake and presses the ground floor button. The person should have travelled only five floors but the mistake means that they have travelled three times as far.

   Which floor number did the person press by mistake?

   Explain your answer by showing your calculation.

# Unit 10
# Shapes and equations

## Lesson 1  Hidden shapes

On the back of these two cards identical polygons have been drawn.

To help us work out what the hidden polygon is we have some information.

> *The number on each card is multiplied by the number of sides on the polygon.*
>
> *The two products added together give 63.*

$(4 \times ?) + (5 \times ?) = 63$

The shape has 7 sides, so it is a heptagon.

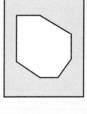

These two cards have another polygon drawn on their backs.

> *The number on each card is multiplied by the number of sides on the polygon.*
>
> *The two products added together give 48.*

$(5 \times ?) + (3 \times ?) = 48$

Use algebra to help solve the problem.
Let the number of sides be *s*.
This gives:

$5s + 3s = 48$
so   $8s = 48$
and   $s = 6$

The shape has 6 sides. It is a hexagon.

To solve the equation you could use inverses, or draw a number machine:

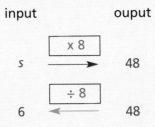

input                    ouput

x 8

s  ──────▶  48

÷ 8

6  ◀──────  48

## Activity

**1.** Imagine two cards each with different numbers on the front but the same polygon drawn on the back.

3  4

The number on the front of each card is multiplied by the number of sides of the shape on the back.
The products from the two cards are then added to make 56.
Form and solve an equation which will help you work out the polygon drawn on the back of these cards. Check your solution.

**2.** Imagine three cards each with different numbers on the front but the same polygon drawn on the back.

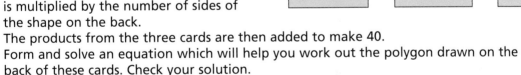

1  5  2

The number on the front of each card is multiplied by the number of sides of the shape on the back.
The products from the three cards are then added to make 40.
Form and solve an equation which will help you work out the polygon drawn on the back of these cards. Check your solution.

## Challenge

**3.** Imagine three cards each with different numbers on the front but the same polygon drawn on the back.

2  3  6

The number on the front of each card is multiplied by the number of sides of the shape on the back.
The products from the three cards are then added to make 44.
Form and solve an equation which will help you work out the polygon drawn on the back of these cards. Check your solution.

# Unit 10
# Shapes and equations

## Lesson 2  Shape puzzles

Five copies of the same polygon are drawn on a page. The polygons are touching so that 4 of the sides are each shared by 2 polygons. There are 16 sides drawn on the page.

How can we use algebra to find out what the polygon is?

Let $n$ stand for the unknown number of sides of the polygon.

We know that there are 5 polygons, so their total number of sides is $5n$.

We know that 4 of the sides are each shared between 2 polygons because the polygons are touching, and there are 16 sides drawn altogether on the page, so a possible equation is:

$$5n - 4 = 16$$

Solving this equation gives $n = 4$.

The polygon must be a quadrilateral but we would need more information to find out which type of quadrilateral it is. Possible diagrams are:

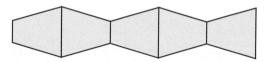 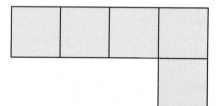

## Activity

1.  4 polygons are drawn on a page. 5 sides are each shared by 2 shapes. 19 sides are drawn on the page.

    a.  Choose a letter to represent the unknown number of sides that each of the 4 polygons has. Write an equation to show all the information.

    b.  Solve the equation.

    c.  What is the name of the polygon?

    d.  Sketch a diagram.

2.  15 polygons are drawn on a page. All have the same number of sides. 20 sides are each shared by 2 shapes. 40 sides are drawn on the page.

    a.  Choose a letter to represent the unknown number of sides of the polygons. Write an equation to show all the information.

    b.  Solve the equation.

    c.  What is the name of the polygon?

    d.  Sketch a diagram.

### Challenge

3.  5 polygons are drawn on a page. 4 of the polygons have the same number of sides and 5 of their sides are each shared by 2 shapes. The other polygon is an octagon. 27 sides are drawn on the page.

    a.  Choose a letter to represent the unknown number of sides that each of the 4 polygons has. Write an equation to show all the information.

    b.  Solve the equation.

    c.  What is the name of the shape of the 4 polygons?

    d.  Sketch a diagram.

4.  12 polygons are drawn on a page. 6 of the polygons have the same number of sides. The other 6 polygons are triangles. Each triangle shares 1 side with 1 of the other polygons. Altogether 13 sides are each shared by 2 shapes. 29 sides are drawn on the page.

    a.  Choose a letter to represent the unknown number of sides of the polygons that are not triangles. Write an equation to show all the information.

    b.  Solve the equation.

    c.  What is the name of the polygons that are not triangles?

    d.  Sketch a diagram.

# Unit 10
# Shapes and equations

## Lesson 3  Shape rings

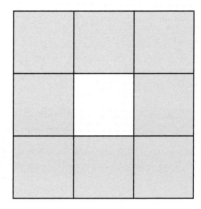

How is the total number of squares related to the number of squares along one side?

This ring of squares can be thought of in two ways.

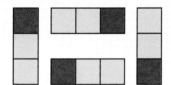  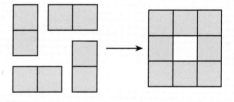

You can think of it as four strips of three squares fitted together, overlapping at the corners. If $n$ represents the number of squares along one side, an expression for the total number of squares is:

Alternatively, you could subtract one square from each strip of three and fit the remaining strips together. If $n$ represents the number of squares along one side originally, $(n - 1)$ is the number left in each strip. So the total number of squares is:

$$4n - 4$$

$$4(n - 1)$$

These two expressions represent the same total, so $4n - 4$ is the same as $4(n - 1)$.

This expression can also be used to find how many squares are along a side of a ring of squares if we know the total number of squares.

Suppose the total number of squares is 56. How many squares are there along each side?

We can write an equation and solve it.

$$4n - 4 = 56$$
$$4n = 60$$
$$n = 15$$

$$4(n - 1) = 56$$
$$n - 1 = 56 \div 4$$
$$= 14$$
$$n = 15$$

## Activity

**1.** Your teacher will give you a copy of sheet **3.7.** Use it to help you find an expression for the total number of triangles in a ring.

 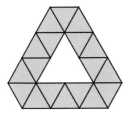 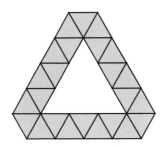 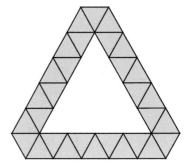

**2.** Your teacher will give you a copy of sheet **3.8.** Use it to help you find an expression for the total number of hexagons in a ring.

 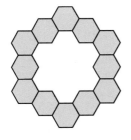 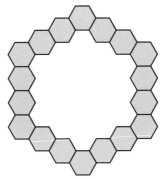 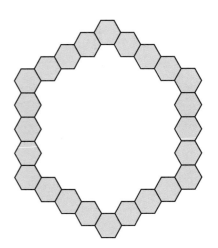

See page 112 for the Challenge.

## Challenge

Imagine that the rings in question 1 are made from matchsticks.

  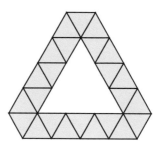 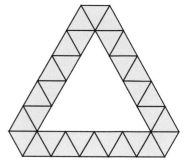

3.  If *n* is the number of triangles along any side of a ring, the total number of matchsticks needed to make the ring is 6*n* – 6.

    a.  A ring of triangles is made with 102 matchsticks. Write an equation to show this information, and solve it.

    b.  What does the solution of the equation tell you?

4.  If *n* is the number of triangles along a side of a ring, then the total number of matchsticks needed to make the triangular hole in the centre of the ring is $\frac{3}{2}(n-3)$.

    a.  21 matchsticks form the sides of the triangular hole in the centre of a ring of triangles. Write an equation to show this information, and solve it.

    b.  What does the solution of the equation tell you?

# Lesson 4  Octagon rings

Octagons can be used to make rings in the same way as other shapes can.
There are several ways to make the first ring in the sequence. For example, each of these
rings has two octagons along each side, but they each have a different number of sides:

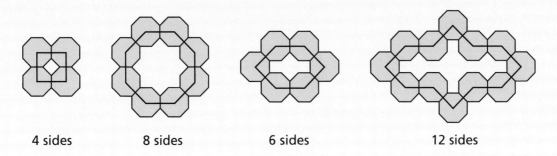

| 4 sides | 8 sides | 6 sides | 12 sides |

To continue a sequence, the number of octagons along each side must increase
systematically. For example, the rings in this sequence always have 6 sides, but each side
increases by 1 octagon each time.

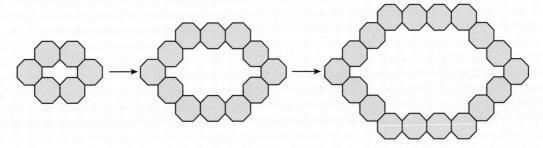

**Activity**

> *You will need:*
>
> *about 60 regular octagons*

You are going to investigate different sequences of octagon rings given on page 114. For each
sequence that you investigate, you must be sure that you can explain how each ring is obtained
from the one before.

1. Investigate this sequence of octagon rings:

2. Investigate this sequence of octagon rings:

3. Investigate this sequence of octagon rings:

**Challenge**

4. Investigate some different sequences of octagon rings of your own.

# Lesson 5  Octagon ring problems

$8n - 8$

In this sequence of octagon rings, the first ring has 2 octagons along each side, the second has 3, the third has 4 and so on.

The place in the sequence is always 1 less than the number of octagons along a side. So the 14th ring in the sequence will have 15 octagons along each side.

If $n$ represents the number of octagons along a side, the expression for the total number of octagons in each ring of this sequence is $8n - 8$.

So the 14th ring has a total of $(8 \times 15) - 8 = 112$ octagons.

Here is another octagon ring sequence:

$4n - 4$

In this sequence of octagon rings we want to find the ring that has a total of 112 octagons. The equation $4(n - 1) = 112$ can be solved using a number machine:

| Input | | | Output |
|---|---|---|---|
| | $-1$ | $\times 4$ | |
| $n$ | | | 112 |
| | $+1$ | $\div 4$ | |
| 29 | | 28 | 112 |

The solution is 29, showing that the 28th ring has 112 octagons.
The solution must be a whole number. If it is not, then no octagon ring exists in that sequence.

## Activity

Your teacher will give you a copy of sheets **5.3** and **5.4**.

**1.**  I am thinking of a ring of octagons in sequence B. If I added 16 octagons to the octagons in this ring, I could rearrange all of them to make the 12th ring in sequence C. Which ring in sequence B am I thinking of?

**2.**  I am thinking of a ring of octagons in sequence E. If I had three of these rings, I could rearrange the octagons in them to make the 36th ring in sequence D. Which ring in sequence E am I thinking of?

## Challenge

**3.**  I am thinking of a ring of octagons in sequence F. If I took half of the octagons in this ring, I could rearrange them to make the 9th ring in sequence C. Which ring in sequence F am I thinking of?

**4.**  Make up your own problem about the sequences of octagon rings on sheets **5.3** and **5.4**.

## Lesson 1  Ratio

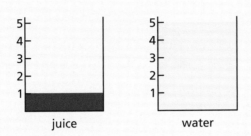

The **ratio** of juice to water mixed to make a drink is 1 to 5 or 1:5.

This means that for every 1 part of juice there are 5 parts of water. It also means that there is 5 times as much water as juice.

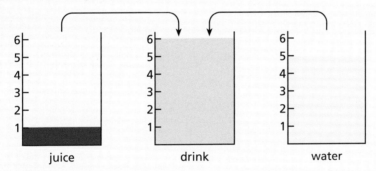

The drink consists of 6 parts.
The **proportion** of juice in the drink is $\frac{1}{6}$.
The proportion of water in the drink is $\frac{5}{6}$.

If the ratio of juice to water in the drink was 5 to 1, the proportions would be different.

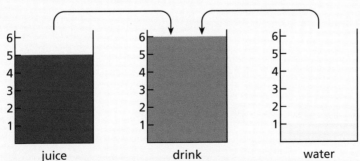

The proportion of juice in the drink is now $\frac{5}{6}$.
The proportion of water in the drink is now $\frac{1}{6}$.

**The order of the numbers in a ratio is important.**

If the ratio of boys to girls in a class is 10:15, this can be written in its **simplest form** by dividing each number in the ratio by 5, giving an **equivalent ratio** of 2:3. This means the proportion of the class that are boys is $\frac{2}{5}$.

The ingredients for a crumble topping are flour, butter and sugar in the ratio 2:1:1. The ratio numbers must be taken in order, matching the ingredient with its correct ratio number.

200g of flour needs 100g of butter and 100g of sugar
400g of flour needs 200g of butter and 200g of sugar

## Activity

1.  The ratio of apples to oranges in a box of fruit is 5:7. What does this mean? What is the ratio of oranges to apples?

2.  Pick out the pairs of equivalent ratios from this list:

    1:2      3:4      4:3      6:8      5:20      12:9      10:20      1:4

3.  Jenny and Ben are 5 and 8 years old. Their mum decides to give them some spending money in the same ratio as their ages. She gives Jenny 30p. How much should she give Ben?

4.  Nafisha is mixing paint. To make a particular shade of paint she uses 2 pots of red for every 3 pots of blue. How many pots of red does she need for 12 pots of blue?

5.  The ratio of black bricks to red bricks in a garden path is 1 to 3. What fraction of the path is black?

6.  What is the ratio of red squares to white in this repeating pattern?

## Challenge

7.  Use squares and equilateral triangles to design a simple pattern in which there are twice as many triangles as squares. The sides of the triangles should be the same length as the sides of the squares. Join corners to corners and try not to leave any gaps. You could do this on isometric paper.

# Lesson 2  Sharing out in proportion

Alice gives twenty sweets to Jo and James in the ratio 2:3.

For every 2 sweets that Jo gets, James gets 3 sweets.

**Equal shares method**

Jo has 2 pockets and James has 3 pockets.
Alice shares the sweets equally into the pockets.

Altogether there are 5 pockets.

20 ÷ 5 = 4, so there are 4 sweets in each pocket.

Jo's share is 2 x 4 = 8.

James' share is 3 x 4 = 12.

A ratio of 8:12 is the same as 2:3.

**Make a start method**

Alice gives 2 sweets to Jo and 3 sweets to James.

5 sweets have now been given out.

Alice repeats the process until all the sweets have been given out.

20 ÷ 5 = 4

The process has to be repeated 4 times, so Jo will get 4 x 2 = 8 sweets and James will get 4 x 3 = 12 sweets.

## Activity

> *You will need:*
>
> *different sizes of pieces of paper (including A4) and old greetings cards*

1. A grape drink is made by diluting 1 part of grape cordial with 6 parts of water. What fraction of the diluted drink is water?

2. One-quarter of the children in class 3 wear glasses.

   a. What is the ratio of children who wear glasses to those who don't?

   b. There are 28 children in the class. How many wear glasses?

3. Asmat is going to plant a flower bed with 2 colours of tulip, yellow and purple, in the ratio 3 to 5. He has bought a total of 24 tulip bulbs. How many of these are yellow?

4. A large section of tiling is made from squares and equilateral triangles in the ratio 1:2. If 120 tiles are used in all, what is the number of square tiles?

5. Divide 360° into two parts in the ratio 4:5.

## Challenge

6. Would you receive more if you got the larger portion of a 4:1 share of £45 or the smaller portion of a 3:7 share of £100? Explain your reasoning.

## Lesson 1  Which is it?

The questions in this activity can be solved using a variety of mathematical methods.

You may use a calculator to help you answer the questions.

If you do not have a calculator, you should make an estimate of the answer and write down the calculation you would carry out to find the correct answer.

**It is important to be able to explain how you reached your answer, so make sure you write down all your working out.**

### Activity

1. A 250g block of butter costs 89p.
   How much is that for each gram?

2. A barrel of pebbles in a garden centre contains 35kg.
   The price of the barrel is £89. How much is this for
   one kilogram of the pebbles?

3. A charity organised a 5.2 kilometres fun-run.
   It took Jane 29 minutes to run the course.
   How far did she run each minute on average?

### Challenge

4. How many bottles each containing 0.3 litres can you fill from a jug holding 4 litres?

5. Maria's car cost £4500 when she bought it.
   Maria is selling it for 0.6 of what it
   cost then. How much is she asking for the car?

When you have answered all the questions, join up with a partner to compare your answers and agree on a correct solution and method.

## Lesson 2  What was the question?

Aarti is making candles for a stall at the school fair.

Using this bag of wax granules, Aarti can make 13 tall candles or 115 miniature candles.

The tall candles sell for £1.45 each and the miniature candles sell for 18p each.

### Activity

In this activity you are given some calculations that Aarti worked out. Try to work out what each one was designed to find out:

*   work on your own, writing down your ideas

*   join up with a partner and agree on a solution.

**1.**  51 x 6          **2.** 51 ÷ 1.5          **3.** 1.5 ÷ 51          **4.** 13 x 1.45

**5.**  1.5 ÷ 13          **6.** 13 ÷ 115          **7.** 1.5 ÷ 115

# Lesson 3  Find the answer

This activity will help you improve your ability to reason in a logical way.

Making up questions so that they can be understood will also improve your communication skills.

## Activity

Make up two different questions, each using two of the quantities written inside this bubble.

**The answers to your questions must also be in the list in the bubble.**

£12

£0.25 for 1kg

12kg

£3

£4 for 1kg

3kg

## Challenge

£8 for 1kg

£40

£8

0.625 kilogram

£5

1.6kg

£5 for each kilogram

Make up two different questions, each using two of the quantities written inside this bubble.

**The answers to your questions must also be in the list in the bubble.**

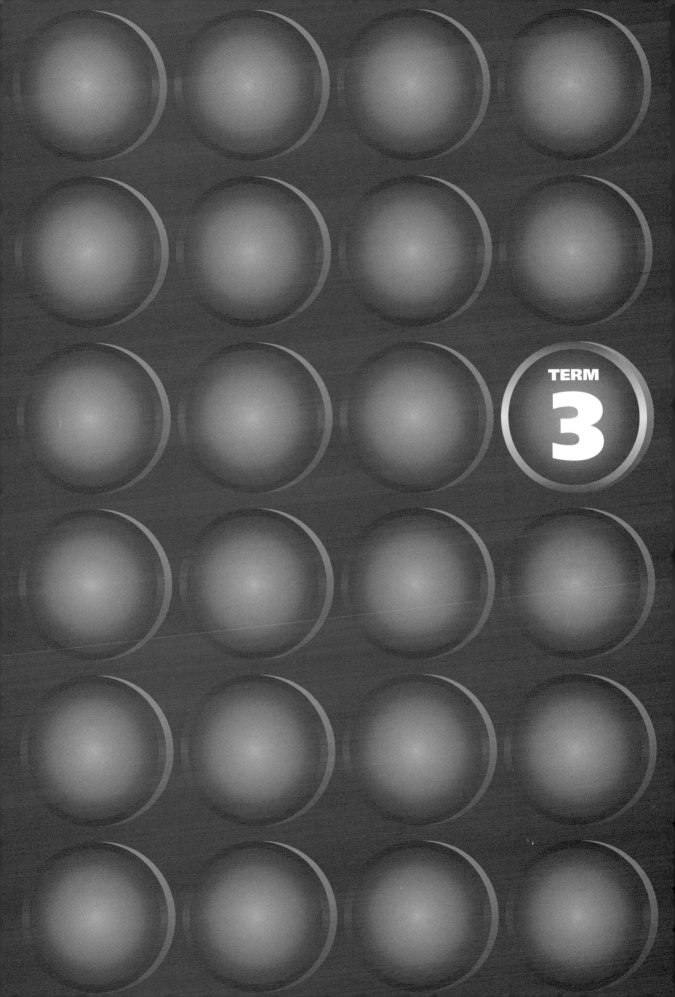

TERM

3

# Unit 1
# Hexatile

## Lesson 1  Let's reflect

When an object is reflected in a mirror line, an identical image is found on the opposite side of the mirror line.

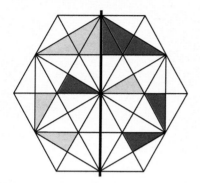

A hexatile is a regular hexagon, and the inside is a tiling of various shapes.

The thick line is a mirror line. Each purple triangle (the 'object') is reflected in the mirror line and each image is shown by a triangle shaded light purple.

This hexatile has two mirror lines.

The purple triangle is reflected in both of these mirror lines and the images are shown by the triangles shaded light purple.

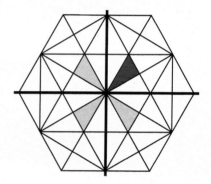

### Activity

1.  Your teacher will give you sheet **1.3**. Shade in the mirror images of the black triangles.

### Challenge

2.  Your teacher will give you sheet **1.4**. Shade in the mirror images of the black triangles. The mirror lines on this sheet are not all at right angles!

# Lesson 2  Symmetry

A mirror line is a **line of symmetry**.

A shape which has a line of symmetry is said to have **reflective symmetry** or **line symmetry**.

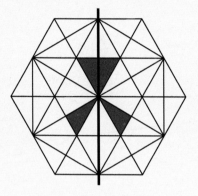
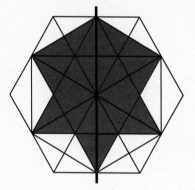

Some shapes have more than one line of symmetry.

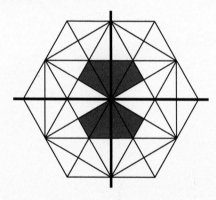
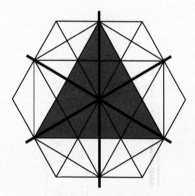

2 lines of symmetry          3 lines of symmetry

## Activity

Your teacher will give you sheet **2.1**. Use it to create shapes with the required lines of symmetry.

# Unit 1
# Hexatile

## Lesson 3  Let's rotate

This hexatile pattern has no lines of symmetry.

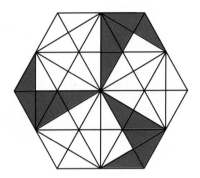

If the hexatile rotates around the centre, the pattern will coincide three times.

The hexatile has **rotational symmetry** of **order 3** about its centre.

Some patterns have both rotational and reflective symmetry.

This 'star' pattern has rotational symmetry of order 6.

It also has six lines of symmetry.

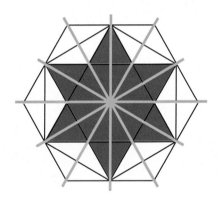

### Activity

1. Your teacher will give you sheet **1.5**. Use it to create symmetrical patterns, some with both line and rotational symmetry.

# Unit 2
# Playing cards

## Lesson 1  An experiment

You are going to conduct an experiment to find out how often each suit is selected at random from a pack of playing cards.

*Remember:*

There are 52 cards in an ordinary pack of playing cards.

There are 13 of each of the four suits:

hearts ( ♥ ), clubs ( ♣ ), diamonds ( ♦ ) and spades ( ♠ ).

The probability of picking a red card is $\frac{26}{52} = \frac{1}{2}$ .

The probability of picking a diamond is $\frac{13}{52} = \frac{1}{4}$ .

When 28 people are each asked to pick a card from a full pack, the number of diamonds expected is $\frac{1}{4} \times 28 = 7$.

So 7 is the **expected frequency** of the number of diamonds.

However, the result is unlikely to be exactly 7 when an experiment is carried out.

### Activity

*You will need:*

*a pack of playing cards*

Work in a group of four to conduct an experiment to find out how often each suit appears when you each select a card at random from a pack and then replace it. The number of times you select a card should be a multiple of 4.

Decide how to record your results. Your results and those of the other groups will be put together, so you must end up with an accurate record.

# Unit 2
# Playing cards

## Lesson 2  Outcomes

When the possible outcomes in a trial have the same chance, they are known as **equally likely** outcomes, for example picking a red or black card from a pack of playing cards.

If the possible outcomes in a trial do not have the same chance, they are not equally likely outcomes, for example picking a picture card or a non-picture card.

Two outcomes that cannot occur together are said to be **mutually exclusive**, for example you cannot pick a card that is black and a diamond.

---

### Activity

1.  Which of the trials shown below have equally likely outcomes?

**Trials**

**A**  Picking a card from a pack of playing cards from which the picture cards have been removed and recording its value.

**B**  Tossing a coin.

**C**  Rolling a 1 to 6 dice.

**D**  Picking a card from playing cards that only consist of the picture cards and recording which 'person' it is.

**E**  Dropping a playing card and noting whether it lands face up or back up.

**F**  Selecting a pupil in the class at random and recording the month in which he or she was born.

**G**  Stopping a car at random and noting the number of people in it.

**H**  Rolling a six-sided dice, with three faces numbered 0 and three faces numbered 2.

**I**  Rolling a six-sided dice, with one face numbered 0 and five faces numbered 2.

**J**  Selecting a counter from a bag containing 3 red, 4 blue and 5 green counters and noting its colour.

**K**  Dropping a drawing pin to see whether it lands with the pin up or down.

**2.** Each event below is obtained from all the possible outcomes for each trial opposite. Write down the probability of each event which is the result of a trial whose possible outcomes are all equally likely.

**Events**

**A** Picking a card from a pack of playing cards from which the picture cards have been removed and getting an Ace.

**B** Tossing a coin and getting a tail.

**C** Rolling a 1 to 6 dice and getting a score greater than 4.

**D** Picking a card from playing cards that only consist of the picture cards and getting a Queen.

**E** A playing card landing face up when it is dropped.

**F** Selecting a pupil in the class whose birthday is in March.

**G** Stopping a car at random with 3 people in it.

**H** Getting a score of 2 when rolling a six-sided dice, with three faces numbered 0 and three faces numbered 2.

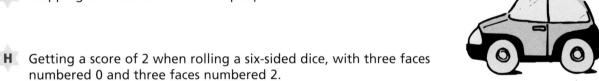

**I** Getting a score of 2 when rolling a six-sided dice, with one face numbered 0 and five faces numbered 2.

**J** Selecting a blue counter from a bag containing 3 red, 4 blue and 5 green counters.

**K** A drawing pin landing with the pin up when it is dropped.

## Lesson 3  Theoretical and experimental probabilities

In Lesson 1 it was calculated that, if 28 people each picked a card from a full pack, we could expect seven diamonds.

This was found using the **theoretical probability** of $\frac{1}{4}$ .

If an experiment involving many trials is carried out, then an **experimental probability** can be calculated by finding the fraction:

$$\frac{\text{total number of diamonds}}{\text{total number of trials}}$$

This will not usually be exactly $\frac{1}{4}$ but should be very close to it.

### Activity

Work in a group. Choose one of the events listed below. You are going to think of an experiment to find an estimate of the probability for one of these events.  Carry out your experiment and compare your results with what you expected to get.

**Events**

**A**  Picking a card from a pack of playing cards from which the picture cards have been removed and getting an Ace.

**B**  Tossing a coin and getting a tail.

**C**  Rolling a 1 to 6 dice and getting a score greater than 4.

**D**  Picking a card from playing cards that only consist of the picture cards and getting a Queen.

**E**  Getting a score of 2 when rolling a six-sided dice, with three faces numbered 0 and three faces numbered 2.

Repeat the procedure for a different event from the same list.

# Lesson 4  Snap

You are going to play the game of 'Snap' in your group. You are to find an estimate of the probability of getting a 'snap' in any one turn of the game by experiment.

The **trial** is selecting a card at random from each of two packs of playing cards.

The **event** in which you are interested is getting two cards of the same value – a 'snap'.

*You will need:*

*two packs of playing cards for your group*

Shuffle and deal the cards equally to each member of your group.  Record the result of each trial as 'win' or 'lose', depending on whether or not you get a 'snap'.

Repeat the game, but this time change the 'snap' event to two cards whose values differ by 1.

# Unit 3
# Percentages, ratio and proportion

## Lesson 1  Protein proportions

> $\frac{9}{100}$ of cooked kidney beans is protein

9 parts out of 100 are protein.

9 per cent is protein. This is written as 9%.

This section of a set of scales shows equivalent values of fractions, percentages and decimal fractions.

From the scales we can see that 80% can be written as a fraction: $\frac{80}{100}$ or as a decimal fraction: 0.8.

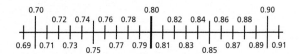

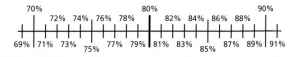

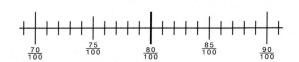

## Activity

1.  Write this list of foods in order of their protein proportions.
    Start with the highest proportion first.
    Use the scales on sheet **1.3** if you need help.

    - $\frac{9}{100}$ of cooked kidney beans is protein

    - 1% of unsalted butter is protein

    - $\frac{1}{5}$ of almonds is protein

    - 100% natural cereal with oats, honey and raisins is 10% protein

    - 150g baked potato has 3g of protein in it

    - 5% of cooked whole-wheat spaghetti is protein

    - $\frac{1}{50}$ of raw cauliflower is protein

    - $\frac{1}{4}$ of cheddar cheese is protein

    - $\frac{1}{3}$ of pumpkin seeds is protein

    - cooked chicken drumstick is 28% protein

    - oil-roasted salted peanuts are 26% protein

    - 4% of chocolate cake is protein

## Challenge

**2.** Repeat question 1 for these foods:

- $\frac{9}{100}$ of cooked kidney beans is protein

- low fat cottage cheese is 14% protein

- 1% of unsalted butter is protein

- cooked chicken drumstick is 28% protein

- $\frac{1}{5}$ of almonds is protein

- $\frac{3}{8}$ of roasted turkey is protein

- 100% natural cereal with oats, honey and raisins is 10% protein

- 8% of boiled chickpeas is protein

- 150g baked potato has 3g of protein in it

- $\frac{1}{4}$ of cheddar cheese is protein

- plain salted crisps are 6.9% protein

- 5% of cooked whole-wheat spaghetti is protein

- 17% of raw oat bran is protein

- 4% of chocolate cake is protein

- $\frac{1}{3}$ of pumpkin seeds is protein

- there is 0.72g of protein in a 72g raw carrot

- 13.7% of whole-grain wheat flour is protein

- $\frac{4}{25}$ of boiled soybeans is protein

- oil-roasted salted peanuts are 26% protein

- $\frac{1}{50}$ of raw cauliflower is protein

# Unit 3
# Percentages, ratio and proportion

## Lesson 2  Equivalence

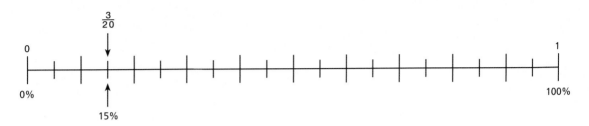

The number line shows that $\frac{3}{20}$ = 15%.

1.  Draw a number line in your exercise book. Show the positions of the following fractions and decimals by drawing an arrow like this ↓ above the line and writing the fraction or decimal.

    $\frac{1}{2}$                    $\frac{1}{5}$                    $\frac{8}{10}$                    $\frac{1}{4}$

    0.6                    0.3                    0.7                    0.9

    Below the number line show the positions of the following percentages by drawing an arrow like this ↑ and writing the percentage.

    80%                    20%                    50%                    40%

    Which of the fractions, decimals or percentages above are equal?

2.  Copy and complete this table.

    | Fraction | $\frac{3}{5}$ | | | $\frac{9}{10}$ | | | $\frac{1}{4}$ | |
    |---|---|---|---|---|---|---|---|---|
    | Percentage | | 30% | | 50% | | 10% | | |
    | Decimal | | | 0.75 | | | | 0.8 | 0.2 |

## Challenge

3.  Write each group of three numbers in order of size, starting with the smallest.

    a.  0.6, $\frac{1}{2}$, 40%

    b.  25%, 0.2, $\frac{3}{10}$

    c.  $\frac{4}{5}$, 75%, 0.7

    d.  $\frac{3}{4}$, 0.3, 40%

    e.  10%, $\frac{1}{5}$, 0.5

    f.  1, 1%, $\frac{1}{10}$

4.  Draw a number line in your exercise book. Show the positions of the following fractions and decimals by drawing an arrow like this $\downarrow$ above the line and writing the fraction or decimal.

    $\frac{1}{4}$ $\qquad\qquad\qquad$ $\frac{3}{10}$ $\qquad\qquad\qquad$ $\frac{7}{20}$ $\qquad\qquad\qquad$ $\frac{4}{5}$

    0.75 $\qquad\qquad\quad$ 0.9 $\qquad\qquad\qquad$ 0.62 $\qquad\qquad\quad$ 0.85

    Below the number line show the positions of the following percentages by drawing an arrow like this $\uparrow$ and writing the percentage.

    35% $\qquad\qquad\quad$ 80% $\qquad\qquad\qquad$ 23% $\qquad\qquad\qquad$ 45%

    Which of the fractions, decimals or percentages above are equal?

5.  Copy and complete this table.

| Fraction | $\frac{1}{20}$ | | | | $\frac{9}{20}$ | | | 1 | |
|---|---|---|---|---|---|---|---|---|---|
| Percentage | | 35% | | 95% | | 60% | | | |
| Decimal | | | 0.43 | | | | 0.85 | | 0.75 |

# Unit 3
# Percentages, ratio and proportion

## Lesson 3  Carbohydrate proportions

**Example:**     Find 63% of 12kg.
63% = 0.63
0.63 x 12 = 7.56
So 63% of 12kg = 7.56kg

Simple proportions can be compared using percentages.

**Example:**     Elm Street has 20 houses and 4 of these are painted white.
Birch Street has 24 houses and 6 of these are painted white.
Which street has a bigger proportion of white houses?
Elm Street has $\frac{4}{20}$ or 20%.
Birch Street has $\frac{6}{24}$ or 25%.
So Birch Street has a bigger proportion of white houses.

### Activity

Make your own set of six 'loop cards'. You may work with a partner.
Use the list of facts below to make up questions for one half of the cards, and
then work out the answers. Add these to **other** halves of the cards, and arrange
the cards so that the questions are next to their answers.

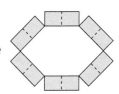

- 15% of a raw apple is carbohydrate
- 3.5% of roasted turkey meat is carbohydrate
- 7% of tinned ripe tomatoes is carbohydrate
- $\frac{2}{3}$ of a strawberry is carbohydrate
- $\frac{7}{200}$ of raw spinach is carbohydrate
- there is 0.8g of carbohydrate in 2g of celery seed
- $\frac{4}{25}$ of raw shallots is carbohydrate
- 10g of seaweed contains 0.96g of carbohydrate
- $\frac{9}{40}$ of cooked long-grain brown rice is carbohydrate
- 24% of a baked potato is carbohydrate
- 25% of crunchy peanut butter is carbohydrate
- in 10g of parsley there is 0.63g of carbohydrate
- $\frac{1}{5}$ of almonds is carbohydrate
- 70g of raw mushrooms contains 2.8g of carbohydrate
- 10% of milk chocolate is carbohydrate
- there is 0.24g of carbohydrate in a 10g cos lettuce leaf

- $\frac{17}{20}$ of honey is carbohydrate
- $\frac{4}{3}$ of a white grapefruit is carbohydrate
- 0.5g of a 50g hard-boiled egg is carbohydrate
- 15g of whipping cream contains 0.45g of carbohydrate
- 20% of tinned sweetcorn is carbohydrate
- 50g of chicken drumstick contains 0.8g of carbohydrate
- 16% of raw sweet cherries is carbohydrate
- $\frac{4}{5}$ of 100% whole-grain cereal with raisins is carbohydrate
- $\frac{1}{25}$ of cooked cauliflower is carbohydrate
- 110g of raw carrots contains 11g of carbohydrate
- 60% of an angel cake is carbohydrate
- $\frac{1}{40}$ of cooked Chinese cabbage is carbohydrate
- there is 12g of carbohydrate in a 24g slice of mixed-grain bread
- there is 3g carbohydrate in 60g of cooked asparagus
- 13% of peas cooked from frozen is carbohydrate

# Lesson 4  Ratio

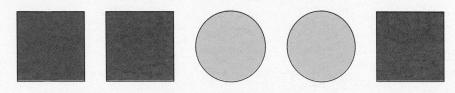

In this pattern there are 3 squares and 2 circles.

The **proportion** of shapes that are squares is 3 out of 5.

This is written as $\frac{3}{5}$, 0.6 or 60%.

The **ratio** of squares to circles is 3 to 2.

If the pattern continued in rows until there were 10 circles, $\frac{10}{2}$ or 5 rows would be needed.

There would be 5 x 3 or 15 squares.

## Activity

1.  To make a steamed sponge for 4 people you need:

    50g of margarine
    50g of sugar
    100g of self-raising flour
    1 egg
    15ml milk

    a.  What would you need to make a steamed sponge for 8 people?

    b.  What would you need to make a steamed sponge for 2 people?

    c.  If you used 3 eggs in a steamed sponge, how much sugar and flour would you have used?

    d.  John has 500 grams of flour to use in a steamed sponge. What else does he need?

2.  A litre of petrol costs 80p. Copy and complete this table.

| Amount in litres | 1 | 3 | 5 | | | | 15 |
|---|---|---|---|---|---|---|---|
| Pounds (£) | 0.80 | | | 12 | 6 | 60 | |

3.  The exchange rate is $1.40 for £1. Copy and complete this table.

| Pounds (£) | 1 | 2 | | | | 70 | 7 |
|---|---|---|---|---|---|---|---|
| Dollars ($) | 1.40 | | 14 | 7 | 49 | | |

4.  A £1 stamp booklet contains 3 first class stamps (27p each) and 1 second class stamp.

    a. How much is a second class stamp?
    b. What fraction of the stamps are first class?
    c. What percentage of the stamps are second class?
    d. How many first class stamps do you get if you buy 5 booklets?

## Challenge

5.  Here is the guideline for the daily numbers of calories and fat needed by healthy adults.

| | Women | Men |
|---|---|---|
| Calories | 2000 | 2500 |
| Fat | 74 grams | 95 grams |

    a. How many calories would 3 healthy women consume? How many grams of fat?
    b. What fraction of a man's number of calories does a woman need? What percentage is this?
    c. What fraction of a man's fat amount does a woman need? What percentage is this?

6.  A Penguin biscuit is composed of the following nutrients.

| Protein | Carbohydrate | Fat | Fibre | Sodium |
|---|---|---|---|---|
| 1.3g | 16.1g | 6.8g | 0.4g | 0.1g |

    a. How heavy is a Penguin biscuit?
    b. A diabetic is allowed 50g of carbohydrate for lunch. How many Penguin biscuits can
       they eat?
    c. If you ate 8 Penguin biscuits how many grams of protein would you have eaten?
    d. What fraction of a Penguin biscuit is fat? What fraction is fibre?
    e. What percentage of a Penguin biscuit is protein? What percentage is carbohydrate?

7.  Investigate the proportion of protein, carbohydrate and fat in different foods.
    You may have some wrappers with you.

# Lesson 5  Equivalent ratios

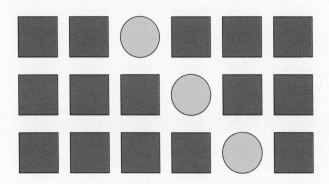

In this pattern the ratio of the number of circles to the number of squares is 3 to 15.

Since $\frac{3}{15}$ is equivalent to $\frac{1}{5}$, the ratio 3 to 15 can be **simplified** to 1 to 5.

This is the simplest way of expressing this ratio.

The ratio can also be written as 1 : 5.

## Activity

> *You will need:*
>
> *set of 28 cubes, ruler*

1. a. Put 10 cubes on your table. Divide them into two piles so that the ratio of cubes in each pile is 2 : 3. How many cubes are in each pile?

   b. Put 20 cubes on your table. Divide them into two piles so that the ratio of cubes in each pile is 1 : 3. How many cubes are in each pile?

   c. Put 28 cubes on your table. Divide them into two piles so that the ratio of cubes in each pile is 2 : 5. Now start again and divide them into two piles so that the ratio of cubes in each pile is 11 : 3. How many cubes are in each pile?

   d. Into what other ratios can you divide 28 cubes exactly?

2. Draw a line like this in your exercise book:

   Write a 2 above the first mark (at the left-hand end of the line) and a 3 below it.
   Count on in twos above the line, recording the numbers above the marks, and count up in threes below the line, recording the numbers below the marks.

   a. Use your line to help you write down 10 ratios that are equivalent to 2 : 3.

   b. Write 10 ratios that are equivalent to 3 : 2.

3.  Draw another line like the one in question 2. Write a 3 above the first mark and a 5 below it. Count on in threes above the line, recording the numbers above the marks, and count up in fives below the line, recording the numbers below the marks.

    a.  Use your line to help you write down 10 ratios that are equivalent to 3:5.

    b.  Write 10 ratios that are equivalent to 5:3.

---

**Challenge**

4.  Look at these tilings of squares.
    Write down the ratio of the yellow area to the white area in each tiling.
    If possible, write a simpler ratio for each tiling.

a.
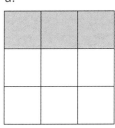

b.
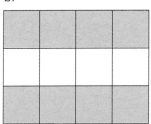

c.
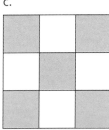

d.
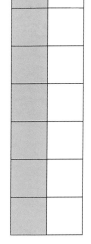

e.
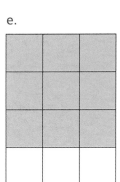

f.
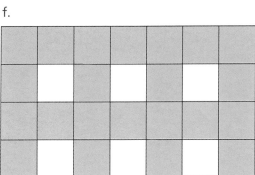

5.  A ratio in its simplest form uses the smallest whole numbers possible.
    For example, the simplest form of the ratio 2:6 is 1:3.
    Write these ratios in their simplest form.

    a. 2:8          b. 3:9          c. 4:12          d. 8:4

    e. 6:9          f. 15:20        g. 30:40         h. 5:5

    i. 10:2         j. 10:100       k. 50:25         l. 6:18

6.  In April there were 10 dry days and 20 wet days. Write the ratio of dry days to wet days.

7.  On the school bus there were 24 girls and 18 boys. Write the ratio of girls to boys.

8.  In the pet show there were 14 dogs and 35 cats. Write the ratio of dogs to cats.

# Unit 4
# Lines, angles and shapes

## Lesson 1 Hexagonal tessellation

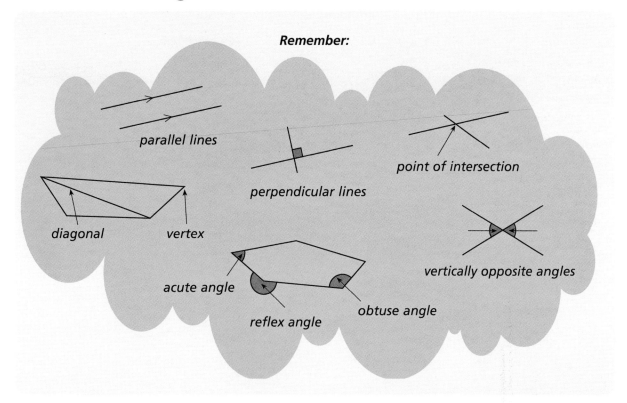

*Remember:*

parallel lines

perpendicular lines

point of intersection

diagonal

vertex

vertically opposite angles

acute angle

reflex angle

obtuse angle

## Activity

Your teacher will give you a copy of sheet **1.4**.

1.  By drawing lines through vertices of the regular hexagons, make the shapes listed below.
    Label the vertices of your shapes with capital letters.
    Use the capital letters to write the name of each shape next to its description in your exercise book.
    You are only allowed to draw lines through vertices of the regular hexagons forming the tessellation.
    Some sides of your shapes may be printed lines of the original tessellation.

    a.  an equilateral triangle
    b.  an isosceles triangle, which is not equilateral
    c.  a trapezium
    d.  a different-shaped trapezium
    e.  a pentagon
    f.  an irregular hexagon
    g.  a rectangle
    h.  a parallelogram, which is not rectangular
    i.  a right-angled triangle

# Unit 4
## Lines, angles and shapes

## Lesson 2  Investigations

This activity will give you an opportunity to improve your computer skills.

### Activity

> *You will need:*
>
> computer with dynamic geometry software

Open the dynamic geometry software.

*Cabri-géomètre II* shows a screen like this:

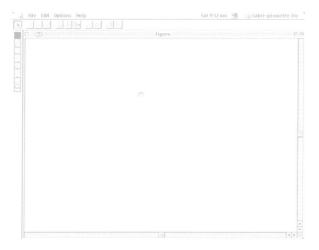

If the icons at the side are not shown, select *attributes* from the *options* menu.

Draw a house like this:

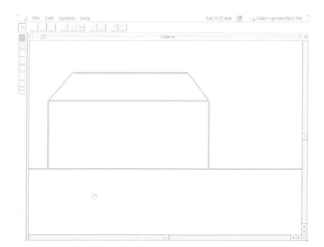

You will need to use the *line* and *line segment* command from the appropriate menu (shown with a line on the box) and the *perpendicular line* and *parallel line* commands (found by clicking on the box with the perpendicular lines).

Mark the intersection of lines with the *intersection point* (found by clicking on the box with the dot), then you can use the *line segment* to join the points.

When you want to hide a construction line, use the *hide/show* command (found by clicking on the box with the sun).

Now you could add another house next to it.

If you use the pointer to select a point you can click and drag the point and change your house.

Measure the angles of the roof. To do this select the *angle* command (found by clicking on the box with cm). Click on one of the lines forming the angle, then the vertex of the angle, then on the other line of the angle. The size of the angle will appear.

## Challenge

Find the sum of the following combinations of angles.  For each combination measure all the angles involved and then use the *calculate* command.

    a.   around a point

    b.   vertically opposite angles

    c.   angles on a straight line

    d.   angles in a triangle

    e.   pairs of vertically opposite angles

## Lesson 3  Explorations

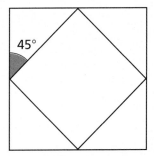

Joining adjacent mid-points of the sides of a square produces a square with edges at an angle of 45° to those of the original square.

Repeating this for the 'tilted' square produces another square. This new square has edges parallel to the original square. The length of its edges are half those of the original square.

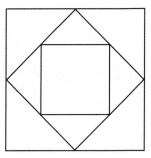

### Activity

> *You will need:*
>
> *computer with dynamic geometry software*

Choose some of the following situations to explore.

For each one you should:
- imagine the situation described
- check what you imagined with the dynamic geometry software
- sketch and write about what you found out.

1. Imagine joining adjacent mid-points of the sides of a rectangle.

   a. What shape do the new lines form? Explain why.

   b. What happens if you now join adjacent mid-points of the sides of the new shape?

   c. What happens if you do this again and again?

2. Imagine joining adjacent mid-points of the sides of any convex quadrilateral.

   a. What shape do the new lines form?

   b. What happens if you now join adjacent mid-points of the sides of the new shape?

3. Imagine joining adjacent mid-points of the sides of any concave quadrilateral.

   a. What shape do the new lines form?

   b. What happens if you now join adjacent mid-points of the sides of the new shape?

4. Imagine a rectangle with both diagonals drawn.

   a. Remove a triangle. What sort of triangle is it? Why?

   b. What other sort of triangles could you have removed?

5. Imagine a square with one of its corners cut off.

   What different shapes could you have left?

### Challenge

6. Imagine an A4 sheet of paper; fold it in half and then in half again to get another smaller rectangle.

   a. Which vertex of the smaller rectangle is the centre of the original rectangle?

   b. Imagine a small triangle cut off this corner. Then imagine the paper opened out. What shape will the hole be? Explain your reasoning.

   c. Imagine what other shapes you can get by folding an A4 sheet of paper in different ways and cutting off different shapes.

# Unit 5
# Statistics and pie charts

## Lesson 1  Collecting data

For this activity you have to think about and decide how you will make particular estimates. You will then make the estimate required for each question. In the next lesson you will **analyse** your estimates.

1.  Choose a specific area somewhere in your school (for example, the walkway between two departments).

    Estimate the number of 1-metre-square paving slabs that you would need to pave this area.

2.  Choose a building in the school grounds.

    Estimate the height of that building.

3.  Which classroom is furthest from your mathematics classroom?

    Estimate the distance from that classroom to your mathematics classroom.

    Estimate how long it would take you to walk between these classrooms.

# Lesson 2  Grouped frequency tables

To make sense of the data collected we have to know what values are representative of the group.

*Remember:*

*The **mode** is the value that occurs most frequently.*

*The **mean** (sometimes called the average) is found by dividing the sum of all the values by the number of values found.*

*The **median** is the 'middle' value – the one which is midway between the lowest and highest values.*

In this lesson you will require the estimates you made during the last lesson and the estimates you collected for your homework. Otherwise you will need a pre-prepared set of data.

## Activity

1. Use your class's estimates of the number of paving slabs as data. Decide on suitable groups to use and then make a frequency table.

   For example, you might decide to start it like this:

   | Number of slabs | Tally | Frequency |
   |---|---|---|
   | 1–500 | | |
   | 501–1000 | | |
   | 1001–1500 | | |

   The **modal group** (or modal class) is the group (or class) that has the highest frequency.

   What is the modal group for your data?

2. Use your class's estimates of the height of a building as data. Decide on suitable groups to use and then make a frequency table.

   What is the modal group for your data?

3. Use your class's estimates of the distance (or time) from the furthest class to your mathematics class as data. Decide on suitable groups to use and then make a frequency table.

   What is the modal group for your data?

4. Use, as data, the estimates you collected for your homework of the length of a line. Decide on suitable groups to use and then make a frequency table.

   What is the modal group for your data?

# Unit 5
# Statistics and pie charts

## Lesson 3  Pie charts

A **pie chart** is a statistical diagram.

Each element in a survey is shown by a proportional area of the circle.

Many facts can be found from this pie chart, for example:

- most people like vanilla ice-cream

- fewer people liked coffee than raspberry

- 26 out of every 100 people liked strawberry.

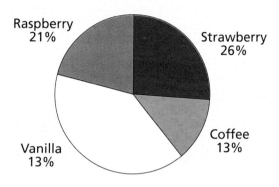

Pie chart to show favourite ice-cream

Raspberry 21%
Strawberry 26%
Coffee 13%
Vanilla 13%

### Activity

1.  This pie chart shows how people voted for the Year 7 school council representative.

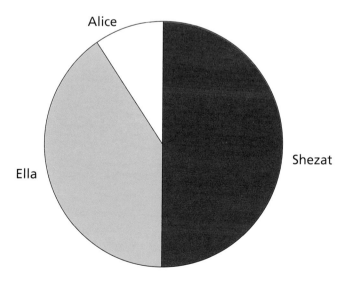

Pie chart to show Year 7 council election

Alice

Ella

Shezat

a.  Measure and write down the angles in the pie chart.

b.  What fraction of people voted for Shezat?

c. If 160 people voted, how many voted for Shezat?

d. Who won the election?

e. Who got fewest votes?

f. Copy and complete these sentences.

_____ won the election with _____ votes.

_____ came a close second with about _____ votes.

_____ got about _____ % of the votes.

## Challenge

2. These two pie charts show the distribution of birds seen one afternoon in a town and in the country. In the town 100 birds were seen and recorded; in the country 200 birds were seen and recorded.

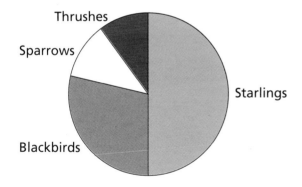

Pie chart to show distribution of 100 birds seen in the town

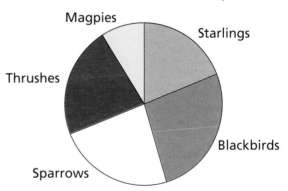

Pie chart to show distribution of 200 birds seen in the country

a. What bird was seen most often in the town? ... in the country?

b. What bird was not seen in the town, but was seen in the country?

c. Which bird do you think is at home in both the country and the town?

d. Which bird is a 'town' bird?

e. Where would you go to have a better chance of seeing thrushes?

f. How many starlings do you estimate were seen in the town?

g. How many thrushes do you estimate were seen in the country?

h. Write a short report for the local paper about the differences in bird populations between the town and the country.

# Unit 6
# Working back

## Lesson 1  Backtracking

*1 think of a mystery number, multiply it by 3, take 1 away from the answer, then I double this number and add 4. My final number is 38. What was my mystery number?*

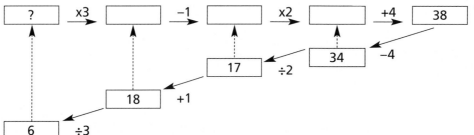

By working backwards we find that the mystery number was 6.
This is called 'backtracking'.

We can use a letter of the alphabet for the mystery number.
If we use *m*, then

| $m$ | | $3m$ | | $3m - 1$ | | $2(3m - 1)$ | | $2(3m - 1) + 4$ |
|---|---|---|---|---|---|---|---|---|
| | x3 | | −1 | | x2 | | +4 | |

So **$2(3m - 1) + 4 = 38$**.

**Activity**

1.  Work with a partner.
    Draw three or four boxes connected by arrows, as shown above.
    Choose a mystery number and write it down so that your partner can't see it.
    Your partner chooses the operation that links each pair of boxes.
    Work out the final number and write it in the last box.
    Your partner has to work out what your mystery number is by backtracking.

    Swap roles, so that your partner draws a row of boxes and thinks of a mystery number and you have to backtrack to work out what it is.

    Keep taking turns to choose the mystery number, using a new row of boxes each time.

**Challenge**

2.  Repeat the above exercise but use five boxes.

# Lesson 2  Starting with the algebra

A mystery number, $x$, after four operations becomes 30.

$$\boxed{\quad x \quad} \rightarrow \boxed{\phantom{xxx}} \rightarrow \boxed{\phantom{xxx}} \rightarrow \boxed{\phantom{xxx}} \rightarrow \boxed{\quad 30 \quad}$$

The number in the last box is represented by $2(5x + 1) - 2$.

So $2(5x + 1) - 2 = 30$.

The four steps to go from $x$ to 30 are:

$\quad$ x 5 $\longrightarrow$ $5x$

$\quad$ + 1 $\longrightarrow$ $5x + 1$

$\quad$ x 2 $\longrightarrow$ $2(5x + 1)$

$\quad$ − 2 $\longrightarrow$ $2(5x + 1) - 2$

Backtracking will help us find the mystery number.

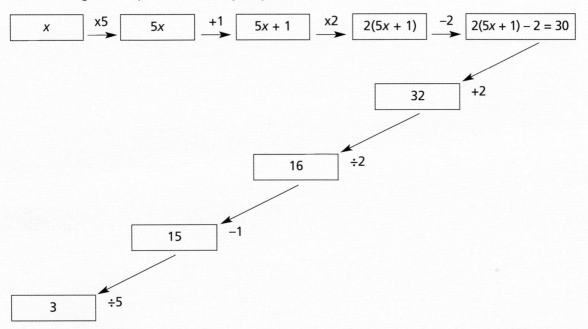

The mystery number, $x$, was 3.

## Activity

1. Backtrack to find the mystery number. Then write, using algebra, the 'story' of what was done to the mystery number. Write in your maths exercise book or loose paper.

   **Hint:**
   - What letter of the alphabet will you choose for the mystery number?
   - What expression will you write in the second box?

   a.

   ▢ $\xrightarrow{\times 2}$ ▢ $\xrightarrow{-3}$ ▢ $\xrightarrow{\times 3}$ ▢ $\xrightarrow{+5}$ | 20 |

   b. ▢ $\xrightarrow{+4}$ ▢ $\xrightarrow{+2}$ ▢ $\xrightarrow{-1}$ ▢ $\xrightarrow{\times 3}$ | 33 |

   c. ▢ $\xrightarrow{+2}$ ▢ $\xrightarrow{+1}$ ▢ $\xrightarrow{\times 3}$ ▢ $\xrightarrow{-4}$ | 8 |

   d. ▢ $\xrightarrow{-2}$ ▢ $\xrightarrow{\times 3}$ ▢ $\xrightarrow{+3}$ ▢ $\xrightarrow{+2}$ | 6 |

   e. ▢ $\xrightarrow{\times 2}$ ▢ $\xrightarrow{+7}$ ▢ $\xrightarrow{+3}$ ▢ $\xrightarrow{-5}$ | 6 |

2. Use backtracking to work out the mystery number in each of the following.

   **Hint:**
   - What happens first to the mystery number?
   - What happens next?

   a. $5(2(b + 1) - 3) = 25$   ▢ → ▢ → ▢ → ▢ → | 25 |

   b. $3\left(\dfrac{n}{2} + 9\right) - 4 = 38$   ▢ → ▢ → ▢ → ▢ → | 38 |

   c. $\dfrac{3(x - 7) + 5}{2} = 7$   ▢ → ▢ → ▢ → ▢ → | 7 |

   d. $\dfrac{2(w + 8)}{3} - 2 = 8$   ▢ → ▢ → ▢ → ▢ → ▢

   e. $\dfrac{3(4m - 9) + 3}{2} = 36$   ▢ → ▢ → ▢ → ▢ → ▢ → ▢

## Lesson 1  Reflection

This lesson will help you to understand more about line symmetry.

You can investigate symmetrical shapes by drawing them in your exercise book.

You can also use a dynamic geometry software package and print your results.

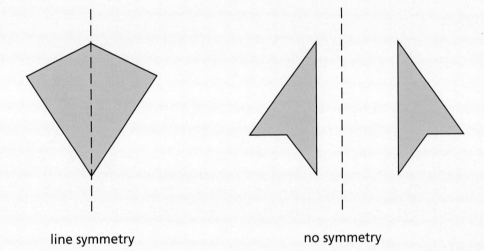

line symmetry                                     no symmetry

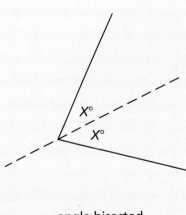

angle bisected,
line symmetry

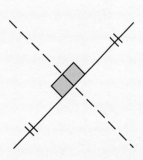

perpendicular bisector of line,
line symmetry

**Activity**

> *You will need:*
>
> *ruler, protractor; or computer with dynamic geometry software*

1. **Reflection**

   Draw a scalene triangle.
   Label the vertices A, B and C.
   To the right of triangle ABC draw a line segment to represent the mirror line.
   Reflect triangle ABC in the mirror line.
   Label corresponding points A', B', C'.
   Join with dotted lines, A to A', B to B' and C to C'.
   Measure the angles where lines AA', BB' and CC' cut the mirror line.
   Measure the distance of A, B, C, A', B' and C' from the mirror line.
   What do you notice?
   Record your ideas.

   Now, investigate what happens when you move your triangle to other positions or move the mirror line.

   What happens to the measurements and labelling?

   Record any further findings.

2. **Bisectors**

   a. **Perpendicular bisector**

   Draw a regular pentagon.
   Draw an irregular pentagon to the right of it.

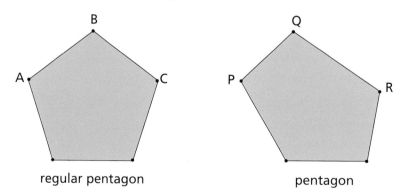

regular pentagon                    pentagon

   Label your pentagons as shown.
   Draw perpendicular bisectors through AB and PQ.
   Measure the angles where the perpendicular bisectors cut the pentagons for the second time.
   What do you notice?
   Record your comments.

b. **Angle bisector**

Draw the two pentagons again and label them as before.
Draw the angle bisectors of ABC and PQR.
Measure the line segments created by the angle bisectors when they meet the pentagons for a second time.
What do you notice?
What is the role of the bisectors in line symmetry?
Record your comments.

## Challenge

3. **Regions**

Draw a square and a mirror line.
Reflect the square in the mirror line.
Count the total number of regions in the diagram of the object square and the image square together.

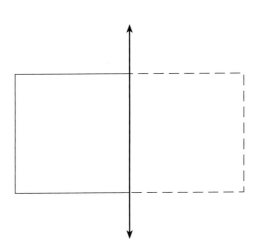

This diagram has a total of 2 regions

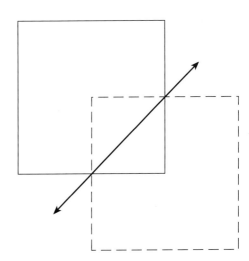

This diagram has a total of 4 regions

a. What is the minimum number of regions? When does this occur?

b. What is the maximum number of regions? When does this occur?

Investigate other regular polygons.

Investigate irregular polygons.

## Lesson 2  Rotation

This lesson will help you to understand more about rotational symmetry.

You can investigate rotating shapes by drawing them in your exercise book.
You can also use a dynamic geometry software package and print your results.

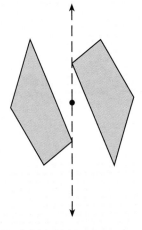

rotational symmetry about ●

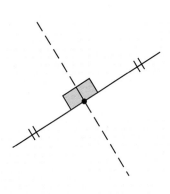

rotational symmetry about ●

It is important when rotating lines or shapes to be careful about the direction of the rotation.

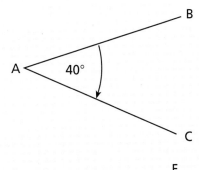

AB ⟶ AC is a **clockwise** rotation of 40°.

This is also called

- a **negative** rotation of 40°

- a rotation of –40°.

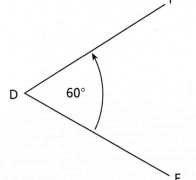

DE ⟶ DF is an **anticlockwise** rotation of 60°.

This is also called

- a **positive** rotation of 60°

- a rotation of +60°.

## Activity

> *You will need:*
>
> *ruler, protractor, pair of compasses; or computer with dynamic geometry software*

1. **Rotations**

   **Part 1**

   Draw a scalene triangle.
   Label the vertices A, B and C.
   Select a point outside triangle ABC and to
   the right-hand side of it. This point will be
   the centre for your rotations.
   Label the point R.
   Join C to R.
   Rotate triangle ABC about point R through an angle smaller
   than 90° and label the corresponding vertices of your new triangle
   A', B' and C'.
   Join C' to R.
   Mark and measure angle CRC'.
   Now draw concentric circles, centre R, that pass through the three points A, B and C.
   What do you notice? Record your comments.

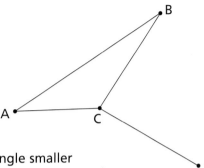

   **Part 2**

   Now rotate triangle A'B'C' about R through an angle of your choice, but smaller than 120°.
   Label the corresponding vertices A", B", C".
   Now rotate triangle A'B'C' about R through another angle of your choice, but again
   smaller than 120°.
   Label the corresponding vertices A''', B''', C'''.
   Now mark and measure the angles of rotation. Each angle of a different size requires a
   different marking.
   Record what you have noticed.

2. **Positive or negative**

   Draw a scalene triangle and mark a point 'R' so that they are placed in a similar way to
   those in activity 1.
   This time label the triangle '1'.
   Rotate triangle 1 about R through –60°. Label your new triangle '2 (–60)'.
   Investigate the results of other negative rotations. Select your own angles of rotation and
   label your new triangles carefully.
   What do you notice? Record your findings and conclusions.

   Complete these statements.

   a. A rotation of –90° followed by a rotation of –50° is the same as a rotation of ____.
   b. A rotation of 270° followed by a rotation of –45°, followed by a rotation of 30° is
      the same as a rotation of ____.
   c. A rotation of 75° followed by a rotation of ____, followed by a rotation of –60° is the
      same as a rotation of –185°.
   d. A rotation of ____, followed by a rotation of 212°, followed by a rotation of ____ is the
      same as a rotation of 28°.

3. **Returning home**
   Draw any scalene triangle.
   Label this triangle 'Start 1'.
   Select any centre of rotation outside
   the triangle.
   Rotate this triangle through 60°.
   Label your new triangle '2'.
   Now rotate triangle 2 through 60°,
   about the same centre.
   Repeat the pattern of rotations,
   each time rotating the newest triangle
   about the same centre, until you have
   six triangles on the diagram.
   Label each triangle in turn.
   Label the last triangle 'Finish 6'.
   As in previous tasks, draw three concentric
   circles to pass through the vertices of
   the triangles.

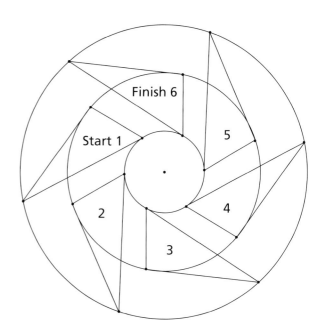

   a. State the order of rotational symmetry of your diagram.
   b. What happens if you rotate triangle 'Finish 6' through another 60°? Give a reason for
      your answer.
   c. Describe how you could rotate triangle 'Finish 6' to land on triangle 4, in one rotation.
      Try to give two different answers to this question.
   d. Describe how triangle 4 could land on triangle 3 in two different ways.

**Challenge**

4. **Patterns galore**
   Take any regular polygon and any point as a centre of rotation.
   Mark this polygon so that you will know that it was the shape where you started this piece
   of work.
   Rotate this shape about your centre of rotation through 60°.
   Now rotate your new shape about your centre of rotation through 60°.
   Continue, until the diagram does not change.
   Now move your start polygon and watch the many patterns you are able to make.
   What happens when you move the centre of rotation?

# Lesson 3  Translations, reflections and rotations

This lesson will help you to understand more about transformations of symmetrical shapes. You can investigate these by drawing them on paper or you can use a dynamic geometry software package and print your results.

A **transformation** can be a reflection, rotation or a translation (or a combination of these). A **translation** does not reflect or rotate a shape. It simply moves the shape horizontally or vertically and sometimes both ways. This is represented by a **vector**.

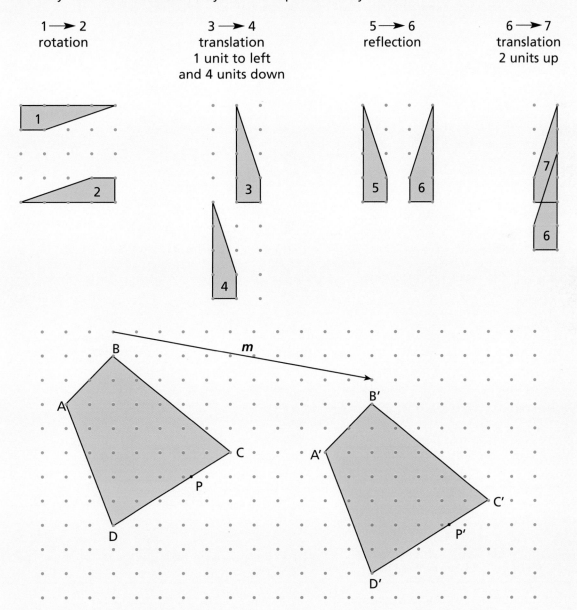

When a shape is translated, every point in or on the shape moves the same distance in the same direction.
ABCD is translated to A'B'C'D' by the vector **m**, that is 11 to the right and 2 down.
So P is translated to P' by the vector **m**.

## Activity

> *You will need:*
>
> *square dotty grid, ruler; or computer with dynamic geometry software*

1.  **The triangle jump**

    Copy these two triangles onto a grid.

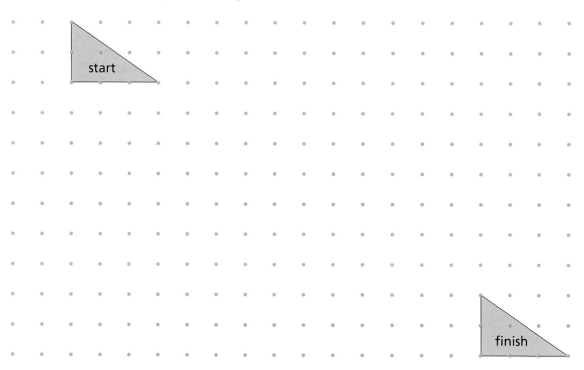

Draw six triangles on the grid that are **exact copies** of the 'start' triangle and that have not been rotated or reflected. Label these triangles 1 to 6.

Imagine that a frog jumps from the 'start' triangle to triangle 1, then from triangle 2 to triangle 3 and so on, finally jumping from triangle 6 to the 'finish' triangle.

Record the moves in a table like the one shown.

Moves to the right are POSITIVE numbers.
Moves to the left are NEGATIVE numbers.
Moves up are POSITIVE numbers.
Moves down are NEGATIVE numbers.

Add up the numbers in the two columns.
What do you notice? Record your findings.

| Units across | Units up or down |
|---|---|
|  |  |
|  |  |
|  |  |
|  |  |
| Total: | Total: |

2.  Combine transformations to create your own designs. Write down the transformations you used and the order in which you used them.

# Unit 8
# Classroom capacity

## Lesson 1  Classroom capacity

How big is your classroom?

What is its volume?

Can you **estimate** its volume?

Good estimating skills are important. They help you to make a mental picture of everyday objects and spaces.

We measure volume in cubic units, and the units must be sensible. You could measure the volume of a biscuit box in cubic centimetres, but you would measure the volume of a classroom or a shed in cubic metres.

### Activity

1. How many centimetre cubes will exactly fit in a metre cube?

### Challenge

> *You will need:*
>
> *your estimate of the volume of your classroom from the class lesson*

1. 1 metre = 10 decimetres = 100 centimetres
The amount of liquid that exactly fills a three-dimensional space is called the **capacity** of the space.
The capacity of a cube with side length 1 decimetre is 1 litre.

   If your classroom was watertight, how many litres of water would it hold?

# Unit 9
# Relationships and graphs

## Lesson 1  Graphical solutions

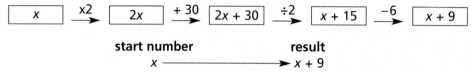

Following the above set of operations,    $1 \longrightarrow 10$

Similarly, following the same set of operations,    $3 \longrightarrow 12$
$9 \longrightarrow 18$

If we start with a secret number, $x$, we get:

$$x \xrightarrow{\times 2} 2x \xrightarrow{+30} 2x + 30 \xrightarrow{\div 2} x + 15 \xrightarrow{-6} x + 9$$

**start number**          **result**
$x \xrightarrow{\hspace{3cm}} x + 9$

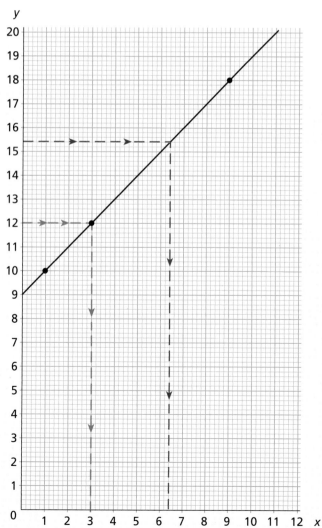

If we call the result $y$, then this result is represented by $y = x + 9$. We can plot points on a graph, using the start numbers as $x$-coordinates and the results as $y$-coordinates, then draw a line through them.

We can use the graph to help us to find a secret start number ($x$) when we know the result, $y$.

When 12 is the result, draw a horizontal line from the value 12 on the $y$-axis across to meet the graph. Then draw a vertical line from the graph down to meet the $x$-axis. It meets the $x$-axis at 3.

So, when 12 is the result, we find that the start number is 3.

Similarly, when 15.4 is the result, we find that the start number is 6.4.

## Activity

Your teacher will give you a copy of sheet **1.2**. Use this to draw your graphs.

1. Look at this table. Plot the three given points (for Vick, Mandy and Ali) on the graph paper. Draw a straight line through them. Use your graph to find the missing start numbers, and write them down.

| Pupil's name | Number thought of (start number) x-axis | Result number y-axis |
|:---:|:---:|:---:|
| Josh | | 14 |
| Louis | | 10.4 |
| Elizabeth | | 16.2 |
| Sunita | | 12 |
| Anna | | 8.8 |
| Megan | | 13.6 |
| Vick | 13 | 24 |
| Mandy | 12.6 | 23.2 |
| Ali | 1.8 | 1.6 |

## Challenge

2. Look at this table. Plot the three given points on the graph paper. Draw a straight line through them. Use your graph to find the missing start numbers, and write them down.

| Pupil's name | Number thought of (start number) x-axis | Result number y-axis |
|:---:|:---:|:---:|
| Mia | | 21 |
| Jamie | | 18.5 |
| Carly | | 20.4 |
| Stephen | | 19 |
| Lydia | | 19.8 |
| Joseph | | 18.1 |
| Rachel | 13 | 22.5 |
| Samuel | 12.2 | 22.1 |
| Amar | 1.6 | 16.8 |

# Unit 9
# Relationships and graphs

## Lesson 2  Points on a line

Pattern A

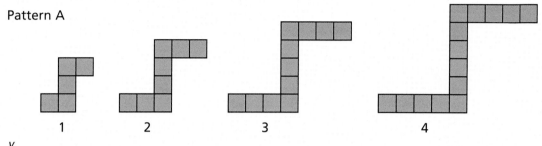

1          2          3                    4

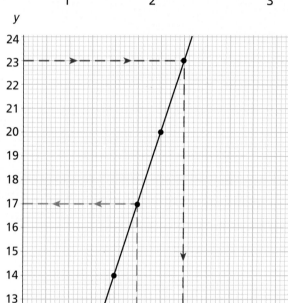

| Picture (or position) number ($x$) | Number of tiles ($y$) |
|:---:|:---:|
| 1 | 5 |
| 2 | 8 |
| 3 | 11 |
| 4 | 14 |

This table connects the position of a picture with the number of tiles in it. We can draw a graph to show this information by plotting the four points and drawing a straight line through them.

The graph shows that the 5th pattern will have 17 tiles.

It also shows that, if there are 23 tiles, this must be the 7th pattern.

## Activity

Your teacher will give you a copy of sheet **1.2**. Use this to draw your graphs.

**1.** Pattern B

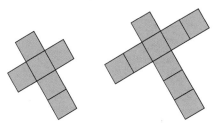 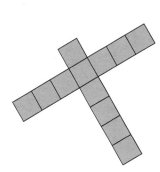 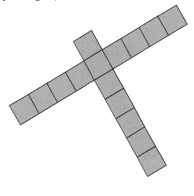

1                            2                            3                            4

Copy and complete this table.

| Picture number (*x*-axis) | Number of tiles (*y*-axis) |
|---|---|
|  |  |
|  |  |
|  |  |
|  |  |

Plot your values for *x* and *y*. Then draw a line through them.

**2.** Pattern C

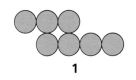  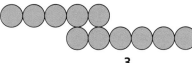

1                            2                            3

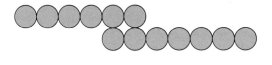 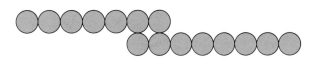

4                            5

Copy and complete this table.

| Picture number (*x*-axis) | Number of tiles (*y*-axis) |
|---|---|
|  |  |
|  |  |
|  |  |
|  |  |
|  |  |

Plot your values for *x* and *y* on the same graph paper as for question 1, and draw a line through them.

## Lesson 3  Investigating lines

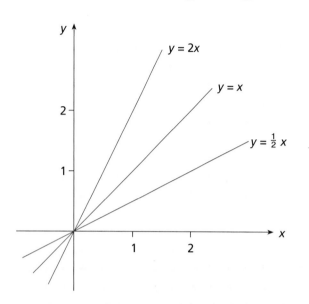

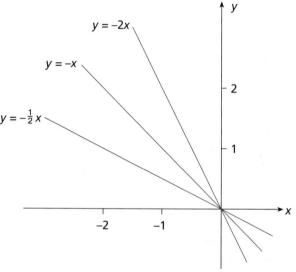

This graph shows straight lines of the form $y = kx$.

Each line slopes upwards from left to right.

As $k$ increases, the steepness of the graph line increases.

This graph shows straight lines of the form $y = -kx$.

Each line slopes downwards from left to right.

As $k$ increases, the steepness of the graph line increases.

### Activity

> *You will need:*
> *graphical calculator (these instructions are for a Sharp EL9600)*

1. Using a graphical calculator, explore the following straight-line graphs.
   To avoid scaling problems, press the reset button before starting.

   a.  To show the line for $y = 2x$, press:

   [ Y= ]   [ ENTER ]   [ 2 ]   [ ALPHA ]   [ X ]

   ```
   Y1■2X
   Y2=
   Y3=
   Y4=
   Y5=
   Y6=
   Y7=
   Y8=
   ```

Press the ( GRAPH ) key.

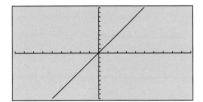

b. To show the line for $y = 3x$, press:

( Y= )     ( ENTER )     ( 3 )     ( ALPHA )     ( X )

Press the ( GRAPH ) key. The lines for $y = 2x$ and $y = 3x$ are both shown on the screen.

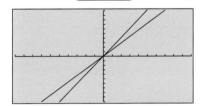

c. To show the line for $y = -x$, press:

( Y= )     ( ENTER )     ( (–) )     ( ALPHA )     ( X )

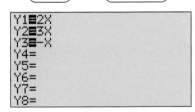

Press the ( GRAPH ) key. The lines for $y = 2x$, $y = 3x$ and $y = -x$ are all shown on the screen.

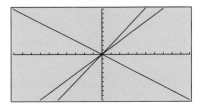

To delete a graph that has been drawn and is no longer needed, go to the 'Y=' screen and delete the equation.

## Challenge

2. Using a graphical calculator, make right-angled triangles from three intersecting lines. Each time, record the equations of the three lines forming the triangle. Try to deduce the lengths of some sides of the triangle.

   a. Try to make a right-angled triangle in each quadrant.

   b. Make a right-angled triangle, then make a reflection of the triangle. Describe the mirror line for the reflection.

   c. Make a right-angled triangle, then try to make the triangle after a rotation about the origin. Describe the rotation.

   d. Make a right-angled triangle, then try to make the triangle after a translation. Describe the translation.

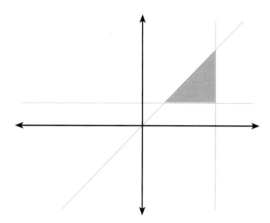

# Unit 10
# Nets

## Lesson 1  Cuboids

A cuboid is an object with three dimensions (3-D).
A cuboid has 6 rectangular faces, 12 straight edges and 8 corners.

A **face** of a cuboid has two dimensions (2-D).
An **edge** of a cuboid has one dimension (1-D).
A **corner** (or **vertex**) has zero dimension.

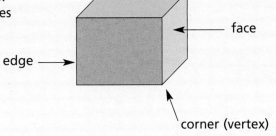

A **net** is a 2-D shape which can be cut out and folded to form a 3-D shape.

With 24 cubes of side 1cm, only one cuboid with different lengths of side can be made. That is the one with dimensions 2cm x 3cm x 4cm. However, the 2 x 3 x 4 cuboid can be viewed in three different ways (orientations), as shown below.  Each has a different net.

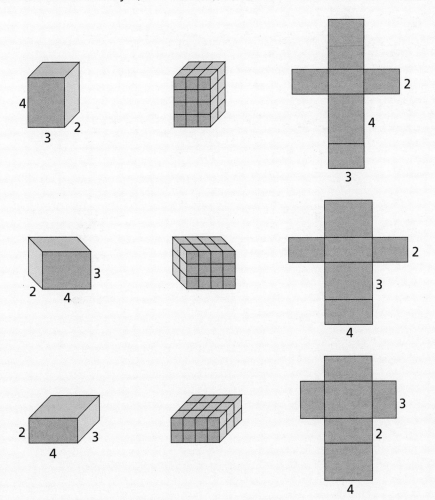

## Activity

> *You will need:*
> *1cm cubes, protractor, ruler, scissors, glue*

1.  a.  Use 36 1cm cubes to build a cuboid with each dimension at least 2cm. On squared paper draw the net of the cuboid. When you are satisfied that you have drawn it correctly, redraw it accurately on plain paper, using a protractor and ruler.

    When you make a cuboid from a net you can use flaps to hold it together.

    b.  What is the minimum number of flaps needed to hold together every edge of the cuboid?

    c.  What shape should the flaps be? Why?

    d.  Draw flaps (approximately 1cm in depth) on your constructed net.
       Cut out the net and make the cuboid.

## Challenge

2.  a.  Draw this net.

    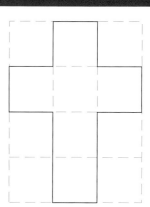

    b.  Using three colours only, colour it so that, if it was made into a cube, no two faces that meet along an edge would be the same colour. Check by making the coloured cube.

    c.  Is it possible to colour the net using only two colours, so that no two faces that meet along an edge are the same colour?

# Lesson 2  Pyramids

Pyramids are three-dimensional objects.

They have a base, which can be any shape, and all the edges leading away from the vertices of the base join together at a point.

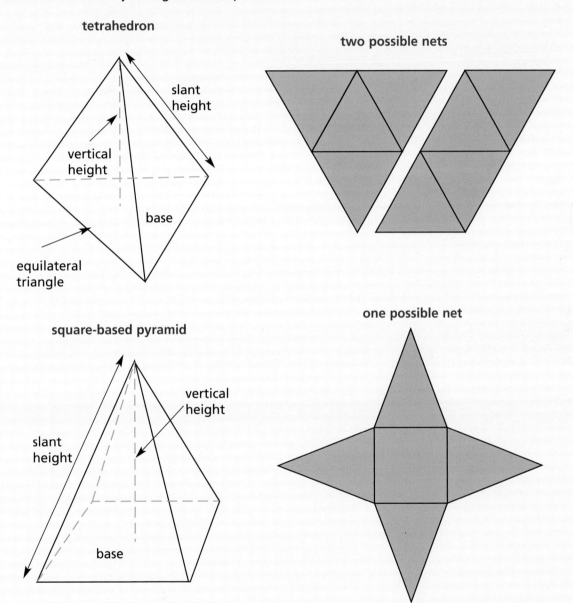

Two possible nets of a  tetrahedron, and one possible net of a square-based pyramid, are shown.

## Activity

> **You will need:**
>
> shape tiles (squares, equilateral triangles, pentagon, octagon), centimetre squared paper
> ruler, protractor, scissors, glue

1.  Put a square and four isosceles triangles on centimetre squared paper.

    Arrange them to make a net of a square-based pyramid.

    Mark on the paper where you have placed the square and triangles.

    Remove the square and triangles and draw the net of your square-based pyramid.

    Put flaps on the net so that the faces will fit together properly.

    Cut out the net and make the pyramid.

2.  Construct four equilateral triangles of side 6cm.

    Cut out them out.

    Put the four equilateral triangles together, to form the net of a tetrahedron.

    Now construct, all in one piece, the net of the tetrahedron.

    Draw all the necessary flaps on the constructed net.

    Cut out and fold the net.  Glue it together to make the tetrahedron.

## Challenge

3.  Choose one of the following polygons:

    *   a pentagon
    *   a hexagon
    *   an octagon

    Use that shape, together with isosceles triangles, to lay out a net of a pyramid.

    Construct the net and make the pyramid.

# Lesson 3  Prisms

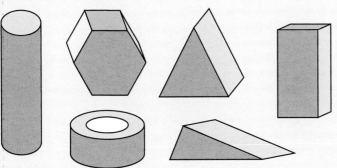

Each of these objects is a **prism** because its **cross-section** is the same along at least one of its dimensions.

This chocolate bar is a prism with an equilateral triangle as its cross-section. It has 5 faces (3 rectangles and 2 equilateral triangles), 9 edges and 6 vertices (corners).

## Activity

*You will need:*

*shape tiles (triangles, rectangles), ruler, protractor, scissors, glue*

1. Work with a partner to design a net of a triangular prism using triangles and rectangles.

   a. Sketch your net and mark on it the length of each line and size of each angle.

   b. Draw your net accurately and put flaps in suitable places.

## Challenge

2. a. Describe two solids that could be used to make this solid shape.

   b. Construct a single net of this shape, placing flaps in appropriate places.

   Make the shape.

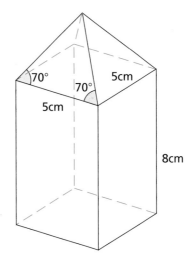

# Unit 11
# Divisibility

## Lesson 1  Sieve of Eratosthenes

**What kind of number?**

*odd*   *multiple*   *factor*   *even*   *prime*

21 is a **multiple** of 3:          $21 = 3 \times$ (whole number, $n$), $n = 7$

5 is a **factor** of 40:          $40 \div 5 =$ (whole number, $n$), $n = 8$

An **even** number is a multiple of 2:          $18 = 2 \times$ (whole number, $n$), $n = 9$

An **odd** number is not a multiple of 2:          $17 = 2 \times 8\frac{1}{2}$, $n \neq$ whole number

A **prime** number has only two factors:          $7 = 7 \times 1$, i.e. itself and 1

A Greek mathematician called Eratosthenes found a method of finding prime numbers. It is called the **Sieve of Eratosthenes**.

All multiples of prime numbers pass through a 'sieve', leaving only prime numbers behind. To find out which numbers pass through, look for the multiples of the prime numbers in turn: multiples of 2, multiples of 3, multiples of 5, and so on.

If the largest number in the 'sieve' is $n$, then the largest prime number whose multiples need to be removed would be $\sqrt{n}$ (the square root of $n$).

**For example, to find the prime numbers from 1 to 80**
$\sqrt{80} \approx 8.9$
The largest prime number less than 8.9 is 7.
Only the multiples of prime numbers up to and including 7 need to be removed.

## Activity

1. Write a short account of how to find prime numbers by using the Sieve of Eratosthenes. Make sure you list the numbers left in your sieve and name them.

2. Investigate what is generally true about the result of multiplying a multiple of 3 by a multiple of 2, such as 9 x 4 or 6 x 8.

## Challenge

3. a. Investigate what is generally true about the sum of two multiples of 3, such as 9 + 15.

   b. Investigate what happens when you multiply, divide or subtract two multiples of 3.

# Unit 12
# Real-life graphs

## Lesson 1  Conversion graphs

**Conversion graphs** are sometimes called 'ready reckoners'. They enable us to do conversions between different units without having to do any calculations.

This conversion graph is used to convert pounds to kilograms, and kilograms to pounds.

Points were plotted for 1, 2, 5 and 10 kilograms and a straight line was drawn through them.

The straight line passes through the point (0, 0) because 0 kilograms is the same as 0 pounds.

Reading from the graph we can see that 4kg is 8.8 pounds.

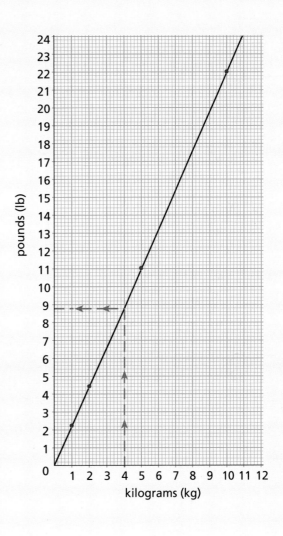

The next graph is used to convert between miles and kilometres.

When conversions are needed within a certain range only (say, 200km to 600km) it is sensible to show a 'magnified' part of the whole graph on a grid (i.e. not show axes all the way from zero).
This keeps the graph at a reasonable size.

The usual way to indicate that only part of an axis is shown is to use a 'zig-zag' line.

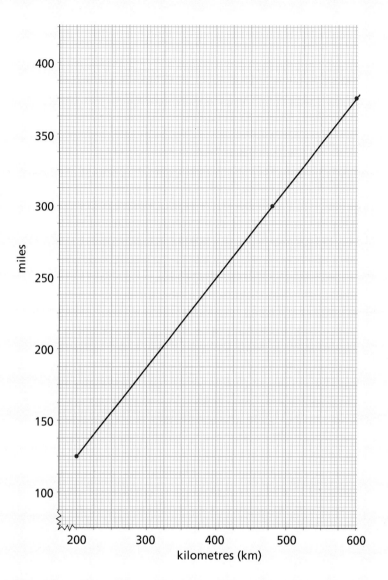

**Activity**

> *You will need:*
>
> *graph paper*

1.  Temperatures can be measured in degrees Celsius (°C) or degrees Fahrenheit (°F). The table below shows four temperatures in degrees Celsius, and their equivalent in degrees Fahrenheit.

| Celsius | 0 | 20 | 70 | 100 |
|---|---|---|---|---|
| Fahrenheit | 32 | 68 | 158 | 212 |

a. On graph paper, draw a graph to convert between degrees Celsius and degrees Fahrenheit:

   - label the horizontal axis 'Temperatures in degrees Celsius (°C)' and the vertical axis Temperatures in degrees Fahrenheit (°F)'

   - on both axes, use 1cm to represent 10 degrees

   - use the numbers in the table to plot four points

   - draw a straight line through the points that you have plotted.

b. Use your conversion graph to convert these temperatures from °F to °C:

   165°F      140°F      66°F      45°F      72°F

   85°F      200°F      125°F      55°F      100°F

c. Use your conversion graph to convert these temperatures from °C to °F:

   15°C      25°C      38°C      67°C      74°C

   80°C      45°C      34°C      56°C      92°C

# Unit 12
# Real-life graphs

## Lesson 2  Graphing experimental data

Sometimes you have results of a survey or an experiment that you have done, which you want to plot on a graph. You may want to see how two quantities are related to each other. In real-life situations, events do not always work out as expected, and graphs may not look exactly as we expect them to. You need to be able to interpret the graph and understand what it means.

It is important to think about the following points.

- Does the scale start at zero? If not, why not?
- Do all the points lie on a straight line? If not, why not?
- Can the graph be continued indefinitely? If not, why not?

### Activity

> *You will need:*
>
> *graph paper*

1. Some pupils held a toy car at the top of a ramp. They released the toy car and measured the distance that it travelled along the floor.

   Then the pupils changed the height of the ramp and recorded the new distance that the car travelled.

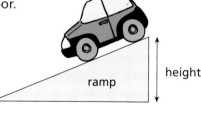

The results of the pupils' experiment are shown in this table.

| Height of ramp (cm) | 5 | 10 | 15 | 20 | 25 |
|---|---|---|---|---|---|
| Distance travelled along the floor (cm) | 20 | 38 | 61 | 80 | 98 |

   a. On graph paper, draw and label axes appropriately and then plot five points to show the results in the table.

   b. Draw a straight line that passes through the five points as closely as possible.

   c. Discuss, and write about, the graph. Include answers to these questions.
   - Why do the points not lie exactly on the straight line?
   - Imagine that the experiment is repeated with the ramp higher than 25cm. Another point is plotted. Approximately where on the graph could the new point lie?
   - Should the graph pass through (0,0)?

# Unit 13
# Historical tilings

## Lesson 1  Wall tiles

Tilings used to be hung on house walls to provide attractive waterproof surfaces.

Here is an example of a historical tiling.

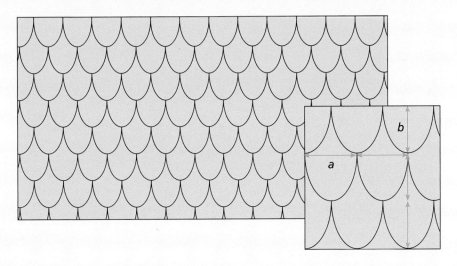

If we know the width, *a*, of a tile and the number of tiles in a row then we can work out the width of the tiling.

If we know the length, *b*, of a tile and the number of rows of tiles on the wall, then we can work out the height of the tiling.

---

### Activity

1.  For the tiling shown above, calculate the missing entries in the following table.
    Copy and complete the table.

| Width of tile, *a* | Visible length of tile, *b* | Number of tiles in in a row | Number of rows | Width of tiling | Height of tiling | Total area of tiling | Visible number of tiles | Area of a tile |
|---|---|---|---|---|---|---|---|---|
| 8cm | 12cm | 100 | 100 | | | | | |
| 9cm | 20cm | 1000 | 100 | | | | | |
| | | 1000 | 10 | 6m | 90cm | | | |
| | | 1000 | 100 | 50m | 7cm | | | |

2. Add two blank rows to your table. Choose your own values to put in some of the columns of these rows, and fill in the remaining missing entries.

### Activity

3. For the tiling shown below, calculate the missing entries in the following table. Copy and complete the table.

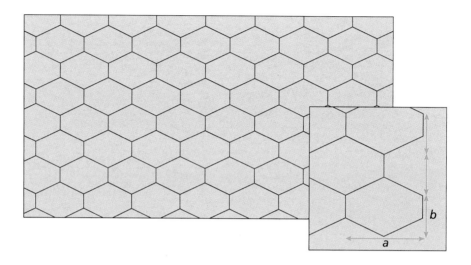

| Width of tile, a | Visible length of tile, b | Number of tiles in in a row | Number of rows | Width of tiling | Height of tiling | Total area of tiling | Visible number of tiles | Area of a tile |
|---|---|---|---|---|---|---|---|---|
| 14.5cm | 7.2cm | 100 | 10 | | | | | |
| | | 100 | 1000 | 880cm | 38m | | | |

# Lesson 2  Floor tiles

This Victorian floor tiling is made up of repeated translations of the 'unit' that is highlighted. This 'unit' has 16 tiles altogether.

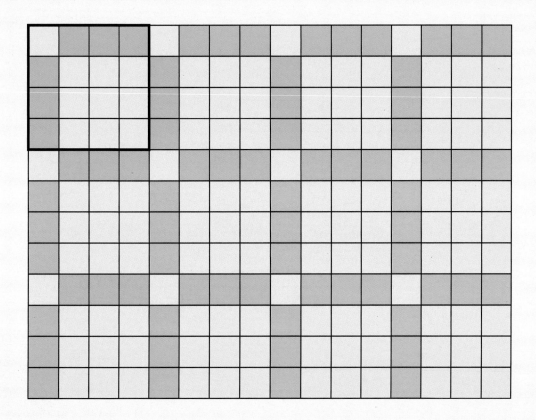

In this unit there are 6 blue tiles.

In four units there are (6 x 4) = 24 blue tiles.

In *a* units there would be (6 x *a*) = 6*a* blue tiles.

For a tiling made with 42 blue tiles, an equation can be made:    $6a = 42$
$a = 7$

This solution tells us that the tiling is made with 7 'units'.

Imagine a tiling made of a number of units and an extra row of tiles. There are 40 blue tiles altogether in the tiling, there are 4 blue tiles in a unit and 8 blue tiles in the additional row.

We can write an equation to show this:

$$4a + 8 = 40$$
$$4a = 32$$
$$a = 8$$

So there are 8 units in the tiling.

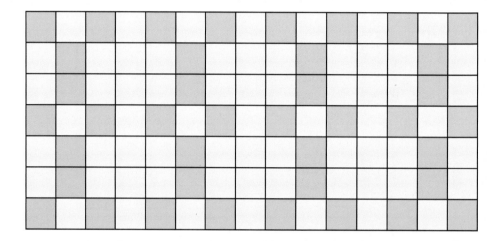

**Activity**

*You will need:*

*squared paper*

1. Using squared paper, create your own floor tiling, with each unit containing 4 black and 2 white tiles.

2. Create a tiling that matches each of these equations:

   - $5x = 20$

   - $3x = 24$

**Challenge**

1. Using squared paper, create your own floor tiling to match this equation:

   - $4x + 4 = 60$

# Lesson 3  Roman mosaics

In 1979, at Fishbourne Roman Palace in Sussex, a black and white mosaic was discovered when another mosaic, which had been laid over it, was lifted. The lower mosaic consisted of 16 equal-sized squares, each with a different geometrical mosaic design in it. One of them is shown below.

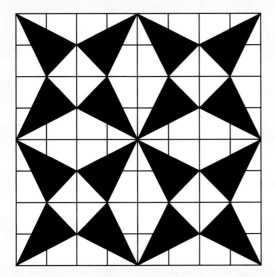

In each block of 4 small squares (a 2-by-2 square), the equivalent of $2\frac{1}{2}$ small squares is white and $1\frac{1}{2}$ squares is black.

$1\frac{1}{2}$ out of 4 is the same as 3 out of 8.

So, $\frac{3}{8}$ of the 2-by-2 block of small squares is black.

Since the whole large square is composed of sixteen 2-by-2 blocks (each with $\frac{3}{8}$ shaded black), $\frac{3}{8}$ of the whole square is black.

The pattern in each 4-by-4 square could be produced by 4 consecutive rotations of a 2-by-2 square about the centre of the 4-by-4 square. The whole pattern could then be produced by reflection in the vertical line through the centre of the whole square followed by reflection in the horizontal line through the square.

Here are two more examples of mosaic tiles:

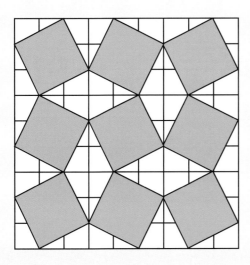
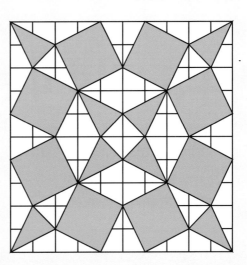

## Activity

Your teacher will give you a copy of sheet **3.3**.

Roman meander border patterns have been found at Fishbourne Roman Palace and in the Romano-British city at St Albans.

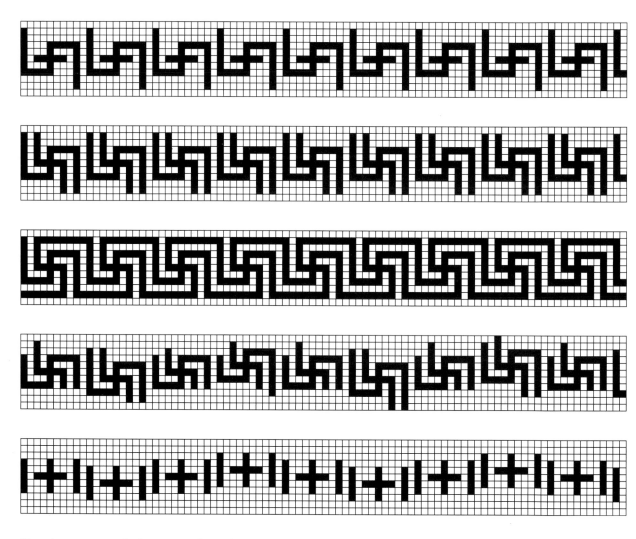

Use the same techniques used on these patterns to create meander border patterns of your own on squared paper.

Do not copy any of the ones shown here.